NT
NATIONAL
THEATRE
PLAYS

OLD MOVIES

A Play
by

BILL BRYDEN

HEINEMANN
in association with the National Theatre
LONDON

Heinemann Educational Books Ltd
LONDON EDINBURGH MELBOURNE TORONTO
JOHANNESBURG NEW DELHI AUCKLAND
SINGAPORE HONG KONG NAIROBI
IBADAN KUALA LUMPUR KINGSTON

ISBN
0 435 23141 3

Published by
Heinemann Educational Books Ltd
48 Charles Street, London W1X 8AH
Set in 10/11 Garamond by
Spectrum Typesetting, London
and printed in Great Britain by
Biddles of Guildford

**For
E.G.**

'My God!' she exclaimed. 'You wrote all these books? I took you for a bookie!'

'They did in Mississippi too,' said William Faulkner, with quiet amusement.

Faulkner — a biography: Joseph Blotner

'Reagan for President!'

'No!' said the wise old movie mogul. 'Spencer Tracy for President. Reagan for best friend!'

Anon

'A good laugh may not be much but it's all some people get in this cockeyed caravan. Boy!'

Sullivan's Travels — Preston Sturges

THE CHARACTERS AND
CAST OF FIRST LONDON PRODUCTION

Old Movies was first presented by the National Theatre Company at the Cottesloe Theatre on 16 June, 1977. The cast was as follows:

Walter F. Bickmore	E. G. Marshall
Christopher West	Kenneth Cranham
William Ford	Fulton MacKay
Charlie	Trevor Ray
Wendy	Rowena Cooper
Agneta	Deborah Fallender
Ralph Rinzler	Glyn Grain
Gendarmes	Chris Hunter
	Olu Jacobs
Director	Bill Bryden
Designer	Geoffrey Scott
Lighting	Peter Radmore
Stage Manager	John Caulfield
Deputy Stage Manager	Frank Nealon
Assistant Stage Managers	Sally Blake
	Fiona Davie

ACT ONE

SCENE ONE

A suite in an expensive hotel in Paris. A large main room with doors to bedrooms off. Ritzy furniture.

Walter F. Bickmore *is on the telephone. He is an American movie producer in his sixties. He wears an open necked shirt, expensive razor-creased slacks that are slightly too short, Italian shoes and Dior glasses. He has very short hair. He does not smoke a fat cigar. Well — not yet.*

Bickmore *(deliberately, as if talking to an idiot)*: Hello! Allo Parleyvooze English? Bickmore. Walter F. Bickmore. I want to speak to the man in charge. No, I don't want anybody else rippin' me off, I want the big chief. . . . Chef de Aero-Porto. Si? Charles de Gaulle. Okay? *(Drily)* Ha ha. Wise guy. I know I can't speak to *him*. Listen. Has the flight from New York arrived yet? Pan am?

> **Christopher West** *enters from a bedroom. He is an English playwright of about thirty. Long hair but doesn't suit it. He wears glasses. He's nice, enthusiastic, casually dressed.*

Bickmore *(urgent)*: That him?

Chris: No. Western Union. Another cable. *(Holds up cable)*

Bick: Shoot!

Chris *(reads)*: 'Plane looks held together by elastic bands. Stop. Risking it to be with you. Stop. Bread shops closed. Please advise. Ford.'

Bick: What if it crashed?

Chris: He's only *(looks at his watch)* . . . a couple of hours. He knows Paris. Maybe he's . . . a la recherche. . . .

Bick *(not really listening):* What?

Chris: Proust.

Bick: I'll stick to vodka tonic.

> **Christopher** *smiles. He moves to the drinks cabinet. Pours drinks. Creme de menthe for himself.*

Bick *(on phone):* It landed? Two hours ago! Did everyone get out? Of course I'm serious. Listen, Frog, you don't know this guy. Have they checked the airplane? It's gone! Where? It's on its way to *where?* Stockholm Sweden? *(Pause)* And I know it's in Sweden, Frog-schmuck. But was he *on* it when it left for there? Listen to me, the guy I'm talking about is a *vee eye pee* I'm paying a whole lot of dough for him and I want him here in Paris France not in Stockholm Sweden.

Chris *(giving drink):* He must have a lot of friends in Stockholm.

Bick: Kid, you shut up, hear? *(to the world)* Why is everyone against me? *(To phone)* I wasn't talking to *you.* I know you was trying to help. So he's not on his way to Stockholm. As far as we *know.* 'Have you got a superior? I know *you've* got a superior. Look. Is there a bar at the airport? Look; listen. Do me a favour. Page all the bars *in* the airport and all the bars within walking distance *from* the airport. You hear? **William Ford.** Tell him to get his ass over here. You hear? I know he's a writer! He's also a drunk. I.V.R.O.G.N.E. Drunk. *(He hangs up)*

Chris: I thought you didn't speak French, Mr Bickmore.

Bick: When you got Bill Ford on a foreign picture there's a few words you've got to learn in the mother tongue. That's one of them. The others I picked up in the navy.

> *(Slight pause. They drink.)*
> *(with a twinkle)* That Proust alcoholic?

Chris: This is Creme de menthe frapee. Proust was a writer.

Bick: No kiddin'?

Chris *(smiles):* Sorry. I thought. . . .

Bick: We're not all Sam Goldwyns you know. More's the pity. *(Sudden idea)* Is there a safe in your room?

Chris: I don't know.

Bick: Look behind the pictures.

Chris goes off to his room to look behind the pictures.
Bickmore looks behind a Dufy reproduction in the
main room, then goes off to his bedroom.
The stage is empty for a moment.
Chris comes back. He also looks behind the Dufy
reproduction in the main room. Bickmore returns.)

Bick: No luck?

Chris: No.

Bick: Me neither.

Chris: Walt?

Bick: Mm?

Chris: Why do you want a safe?

Bick: We must hide it.

Chris: What?

Bick: The script.

Chris: Don't you want to read it first?

Bick: I don't trust *anyone* to read it, not even myself. What if
he's dead? With Bill Ford that could happen anytime. What
if he's passed out in the john in that plane halfway to
Stockholm Sweden? Huh? What about that? What if his cab
crashed on the way in from the airport. You know these Frog
taxi drivers. They invented motor racing. Why do you think
they call them Grand Prix? If *we* had started it they'd be
called Champeenships. 'Grand Prix' Johnny Frankenheimer.
Lost a fortune. 'They had to do retakes before they put the
damn thing on the shelf.' Ha! If William Ford is dead, he
stops being a drunk, he becomes a genius again. Nobel prize
winner. Poet of the common man and Christopher my boy,
that piece of shit you've been writing all week becomes
priceless. Like a Rembrandt.

Chris: A forged Rembrandt.

Bick: Who's to know?

Chris: I'm to know, Mr Bickmore.

Bick: Integrity. Listen, kid. I picked you up from nothing. A
couple of faggy plays in London in some theatre I couldn't
hardly find and you're coming on with the integrity. I'm
paying you very well.

Chris: Don't think I'm ungrateful.

3

Bick: Don't worry. I'll make you famous. That's what you want. So. If Bill's a goner, 'The Lord' is by *him*, right? *(Slight pause)* Put it on the table where I can see it.

> Chris *puts script on table.*

Chris: Are you really telling me that if he's dead, in that loo, getting even nearer to Stockholm it's a masterpiece and if he walks through that door as large as life, it stinks.

Bick: Yeah. That's what I'm telling you.

Chris: Christ! What a business.

Bick: Don't knock it, kid, and don't blaspheme. We want Vatican bread behind this show. Tell me where else could the son of a poor immigrant hat-blocker end up a millionaire with a Montecristo to smoke, a Rolls Royce to drive, and a Toulouse-Lautrec in every damn room in his house 'cept one?

Chris: Politics. *(Slight pause)* Can I phone my wife?

Bick: I want all the lines clear. Go next door and type an obituary.

Chris: Shouldn't we give him just a little more time?

Bick: Okay. Lie on the couch and *think* about an obituary.

> Chris *moves to sit.*

Bick: How big are you in London?

Chris: Sorry?

Bick: Would The Times of London print your obituary if you said you'd spent his last hours with him?

Chris: They might. They probably would. But that would be a lie.

Bick: Once and for all, Chris. Keep a low profile on the integrity, will ya? Jesus Christ!

> Chris *stretches out on the sofa.*

Chris: Remember the Mormon money, Walt.

Bick: *(laughing, then stops):* Why am I laughing? Do you think God's against this picture?

Chris: You know, Walt. In London they don't believe there are still people like you in pictures. In London there are no people in pictures anymore.

Bick: I'm a plain man. I don't fag around like these new guys. Long hair, trying to look like actors or jazz musicians, smoking dope and talking politics. I voted for Nixon and I'd still vote for Nixon if these Communist newspapermen

4

hadn't blown the whistle on him. He gave me a pair of cufflinks. Look.

Chris: A bit unfashionable, don't you think?

Bick: The President of the United States gave them to *me*. He talked to *me*.

Chris: I think I'd better have a drink. *(Moves to drinks table. Another frappee. Pause.)* I wonder where he is. It's funny.

Bick: What's funny? Nothing is funny.

Chris: His courage. I'm very efficient. I turn up on time. I do what I'm told. I make deadlines. I deliver. I admire his courage.

Bick: You're young. You'll learn. You'll get an image, same's Bill. You haven't even thought of what you look like. Bill dresses like a guy lining up for relief under Roosevelt or whoever was Prime Minister when he drew relief in Glasgow.

Chris: A drink?

Bick: Now don't you start, Chris. If Bill ever does show the only way you'll get Christ crucified this month is by keeping him away from that. I want him sitting chain smoking over that typewriter. *(Sudden inspection of typewriter)* That's okay. It's IBM. He hates Germans and Italians.

Chris: Why do you need me?

Bick: You're my insurance. Also, you're cheap. Bill's my genius. That costs money.

Chris: I've never been paid so much in all my life. I wrote a film in England all by myself for less.

Bick: You've got the best agent. Don't complain.

Chris: He must have been sober sometimes to have written fifteen novels and I don't know how many short stories. You don't win the Nobel Prize by being pissed out of your mind every day.

Bick: How the hell would you know? Do you think Herman Manciewitz was sober when he wrote 'Citizen Kane'?

Chris: Orson Wells wrote it.

Bick: Bullshit. Old Manky wrote it. First half topping up the second half drying out. Sinclair Lewis won the Nobel Prize drinking and fucking, fucking and drinking. Never wrote anything after. That's what Hemingway said about it. Nobody who wins the goddam thing writes a single word

5

that's any good after. *That's* what worries me about Bill, and that's why you're here.

Chris: Can I phone my wife?

Bick: Look. Later, okay? There's a man dying up there in the john over Stockholm Sweden.

Chris: It's very appropriate. 'Nobel Prize Winner dies over Sweden'.

Bick: Look, this is an eight million dollar movie. May be ten 'fore we're through. It is not funny.

Chris: That was a great speech he made.

Bick: Who?

Chris: Ford. When he accepted the prize. *(Quoting with respect)* 'Like the sower with his seed and the man behind the plough, the writer has his trade also. He tills his field and the field yields forth its crop. He is part of the land.'

Bick: Bill writes better than that for money. Get me a vodka tonic. I defy my ulcer.

Chris *(by the drinks):* There's no ice.

Bick *(as if in one sentence):* Ring down for some. No, Better not. *(Picks up the phone)* Hello. Room Service. No, listen. We may be having a very important call through from Sweden so don't leave the phone. Tell somebody down there to bring some ice up but the call's more important. Look, forget the goddamned ice. Somebody's got to be sober. Just stand by for Stockholm! Ten Four! *(Hangs up)* Look go easy kid. If Bill's okay and just sightseeing I want some time out of both of you. Charlie's coming tomorrow. He's got three new faces in England tied up. Like to show him a few pages. There's one of them going to test for Jesus.

Chris: Which one?

Bick: I don't know. Young guys from the theatre. Unknowns.

Chris: I bet I know them.

Bick: Look, if Mr and Mrs America in Altoona, Pennsylvania don't know them they're unknowns, right? Why am I shouting at you? Christ! There I go again, I wish the bastard would show up. He's let me down before, but usually after a week, ten days. He normally shows up on time to get the drinking started, then a few days later he goes to work on the script. First, he asked me why I'm doing it. You know Bill likes me and I like Bill. Sure, he's a great writer, but better than that, he's a great guy.

Chris leans back on the sofa.

Chris   'A great writer and a great guy', Walter F. Bickmore, talking from Paris this morning, mourned the loss of one of the world's literary lions . . .''

Bick: 'Zat what it sounds like?

Chris: 'Fraid so.

Bick: I didn't mean it like that. You'll like him, Chris, but I warn you about one thing, if he isn't lying on a slab in a Swedish morgue, that is. Don't talk about writing or plays or the future of the novel, or any of that shit. He lays a fine on you every time you do. Except women. Women can do what they like if they let him in their pants. He doesn't look or act sixty. There's many a kid, grown up now who knows their Mom' was a one time communist student but don't know their dad is a genius.

Chris: He's married, isn't he?

Bick: We're all married, kid. Poor Sarah. You better phone your wife. Sorry I didn't want her here. It's a rule.

Chris: It's alright, I'll wait.

Pause. **Bickmore** *smiles.*

Bick: Don't worry. He's not in Stockholm. He'll be here. In Paris. In a telephone booth. Stinko. Ringing up some 'pal' o' his he balled after some party at Gallimard to launch a novel or a book of poems. He used to tell me he'd always ask her 'Who or what are we launching today?' If she didn't know either he'd say 'They must be launching our lasting friendship'. He's full o' shit.

Chris laughs.

Chris: You're very fond of him, aren't you?

Bick: Yes, I am. I've read pages from him that any other writer couldn't begin to write. He leaves 'em cold. Even the best. It finishes up in the trashcan. He's never faced up to the movie business. He thinks it's greedy. Vulgar. And he's right. He wrote a description of Lake Geneva that was better than the real thing. Trashcan. Bill Ford's a man God has tapped on the shoulder. I just hope we get him on the screen. If we don't, you're it. If you deliver. Otherwise, it's somebody else, but I'll tell ya this; if the entire Writers Guild works on this goddam script Bill Ford's name will still be on it, somewhere. Sure, it's prestige. It's also a bundle of laughs. Here's to him and our backers. The Vatican and Bill Ford. What a team! Sodom and . . . Begorrah! *(He drinks)* Where *is* the son of a bitch?

    Slight pause

Chris *(firmly):* I would like you to read the script. Before he comes.

Bick: I'm sure it's just terrific. We'll wait until he gets here, okay?

    Slight pause

Chris: You think he's going to do it this time, don't you?

Bick: Nope. But I hope he does. He'll try. Always needs money. 'Bread shop's closed. Please advise'. That's typical. I know he's frightened to death that his new book stinks and if he thinks it stinks, it stinks. Maybe he'll take it out on us and deliver. Odds are against but it's worth a place bet. Ford's a thoroughbred.

Chris: Charlie gets in tomorrow. What will he say if Bill's . . .

Bick: Charlie's an agent. What does Charlie know? His job is to deliver a couple of cheap disciples and maybe an even cheaper Jesus Christ. He's not handing out the Pulitzer Prize. Thank God. Look, Chris, I'm no egghead but you write it down, I'll know if it's people talking.

    Chris *rises and moves to the drinks cabinet.*

Chris: I hope we . . . well . . . hit it off.

Bick: Don't worry, kid. You can do the typing.

Chris: I wanted to do a good job.

Bick: Shit. This isn't a good job. That thing Bill wrote about the farmers going to war . . .

Chris: 'A Psalm of David'?

Bick: Yeah. That was a good job. No studio would touch it. No this isn't a good job. This is desperation street.

    The main door opens. **William Ford** *enters. He is carried by two* **Gendarmes.** *He wears a harris tweed suit, rumpled but expensive. A cap on his head, tweed also but not the same. A small red rosette in his* *buttonhole. He is small, neat with grey hair and moustache. Just over sixty. He collapses to the floor. He curls up to sleep as if the carpet were a pillow.*

Ford *(very quietly):* Merci.

Bick: Where'd you find?

1st Gendarme: St. Germain. Ivre.

Bick: I can see that. Why didn't you lock him up?

1st Gendarme: Officier. *(He points to* **Ford's** *lapel)*

Chris: Of course. The Rosette. The Legion d'Honneur. He's an officer of the Legion of . . .

Bick: I know what he is!

Chris: They have special privileges.

Bick: I have a strange feeling we've come to the wrong city.

FADE

SCENE TWO

The suite the following day. Brilliant morning light through the windows.

In the main room, **Christopher** *is typing.* **Ford** *enters from a bedroom. He goes to the drinks cabinet.* **Christopher's** *attention is on him, not on what he is writing. Time passes.* **Christopher** *types louder, his concentration gone.* **Ford** *pours a large scotch. He speaks with a Glasgow accent, impure and a bit anglicised, but exact and strong when he's angry.*

Ford *(at drinks):* Drinky?

Chris: Do you think that's . . .

Ford: Wise?

Chris: Mm.

Ford: *Ab*solutely.

>**Ford** *carefully puts a little water in his whisky.*
>**Christopher** *goes back to his typing. Before* **Ford** *raises the glass to his lips . . .*

Ford: No champagne?

Chris: Eh? . . . No.

Ford: Walt's usually organised.

>**Ford** *sits in an armchair. Pause. He drinks the whisky in one.*

Chris: It's a great honour to be working with you, Mr Ford.

Ford: Don't dedicate it too much. You'll live to regret it. Do you have a cigar*ette?*

Chris: Sure. *(He gives* **Ford** *his Gauloises packet)*

Ford: Golliwogs. I knew it.

>**Chris** *withdraws packet.*

>*(Taking cigarette)* Better than nothing. Least there are no 'spats' on it. *(He lights his cigarette. He needs it)*

Chris: Can I ring down for your breakfast?

Ford: Thank you. Thank you very much.

>**Chris** *rises. Goes to the table. Picks up telephone. He waits.*

Chris: What'll it be?

Ford: Orange juice. Fresh. And champagne. I'll mix it myself.

Chris: No, I won't *(He hangs up)*

Ford: Christ. May I call you Chris?

Chris *(angry):* What are you trying to *do?*

Ford: I know what you're going to say. Older and wiser have said it before you.

Chris: Get your own bloody breakfast. Kill yourself. Go on!

>*Slight pause.*

Ford: Are you in a huff? Do I detect a wee wave of huffiness? I know. I come staggering in here late, supported by the Police and my reputation, with no intention of doing a hand's turn, and then I don't make up for it by crashing into the Pentateuch before lunch. Look, forget breakfast. Couple o' these'll do fine.

>**Ford** *coughs a terrible morning cough.*
>*Pause.*

Chris: Sorry.

Ford: No pity! No thank you. I've still to read what you've written.

Chris: Would you? No-one will read it.

Ford: Walt can't read. You'll find that a blessing 'fore you're done.

Chris: You don't care about the movies, do you?

Ford: Son. I care about who pays me. Too many writers shit on Hollywood. They blame the movies for not being able to write. It's the money to blame. 'I'm just doing this one then I'll get back to my novel.' Some hope. Money makes them crazy. Money erodes their talent. No one has that big a talent. Look, I'm sixty and I'm writing 'that novel' so don't expect me to get too het up about this. *(He lifts the script)* 'The Lord'. 'A Walter F. Bickmore Production'. Could you tell me what Walter F. Bickmore's got to do with Jesus H. Christ, eh?

Chris: We're looking at it from a different perspective.

Ford: Do the Jews win?

        Chris *laughs*

That was a nervous laugh. Have a drink or smoke dope if ye like. I don't care. Where's Walt?

Chris: Buying flowers for Charlie's daughter.

Ford: Who's Charlie's daughter? For that matter, who the hell's Charlie?

Chris: He's an agent. Arrives today to look at the script.

Ford: Wha . . . ? Don't come it! You want me to think about the Gospel according to St Matthew on an empty liver to impress a fucking agent? That's like takin' three years to write a book to impress a critic. Whoorin' bi-Christ!

Chris: What about doing it for a fellow writer?

Ford: Full marks. Pleased to meet you, Chris-topher. *(They shake hands)* What ye done?

Chris: Fifty pages.

Ford: Busy bee, eh?

Chris: Ten aren't bad.

Ford: Modesty we can do without.

Chris: Just read the bloody thing, will you? Nobody will read it.

Ford: I'm sure the agent will be honoured to. . . .

Chris: *You* read it.

Ford: No, I'm sure it's terrific. I saw your play. The one about

11

the gypsies. Can I talk to you about. . . .

Chris: Sure.

Ford: No. It always ends in tears. I liked it. Why should I make you think it's no good? Why should you listen to me?

Chris: I'd love to hear your opinion. Honestly.

Ford: When people say that they want praise. You can't write about the Highlands in a weekend. Trouble is . . . you're no gypsy. Anything but. You were trying to be significant. Meaningful. People want a laugh. They don't want the truth. To hell with the truth. Have a drink.

Chris: No.

Ford: Mind if I do? (**Ford** *pours a scotch*) Look, Chris. It's Paris. Paris! Let's traverse the 'Lemon Streets'. It's yet morning. Many's the fine morning I've seen the Seine from the Pont d'Alma. What are we doin' fucking a porcupine?

Chris *(with a grin):* Sorry?

Ford: Fucking a porcupine? Oh, I wish it was original. A writer told me. Years ago. He was working with Walt or somebody like Walt. Worse than Walt — there's a lot worse than Walt, you know? But it's true. Working for Walt is like fucking a porcupine. It's a hundred pricks against one.

> **Chris** *laughs. Enter* **Bickmore** *from main door. He carries a too large, rather vulgar bouquet.*

Ford: Walt! You look *beautiful*. Listen. Sorry, you were a hazy glint in the corner of my eye last night. You haven't changed a bit. Still on the B12, health farms, saccarine in your tea, and the occasional relief massage, eh? I love the room, I love Paris, and I love you, Walt. All the best. *(Shakes hands warmly)* I've just met Lloyds of London.

Bick: Quit kidding, Bill.

Ford: Insurance, Walt. For the first time you might get a literate script for this show of yours without me putting pen to paper. What are you going to take for it, Walt?

Bick: It's a bit early for me.

Ford: Maybe it's too late. (**Walt** *smiles,* **Ford** *frowns. Serious*) Don't smile like that, Walt. Don't smirk. It makes me feel like a drunk. I hear the agents are coming. Shall I undo my tie, walk up and down, and say 'I've got it' when you give me the nod, go next door and make the noise of furious lying type-writers, so that he'll leave, not wishing to destroy the creative process. Or alternatively, I could make one 'phone call to ensure a pleasant afternoon in matchless company so as not to embarrass *you* and the man from the *Pru*. The choice is yours, Walt, and you've got to choose.

Bick: Charlie's crazy to meet you, Bill. His daughter has read all your books.

Ford: She must have had to. A student, I fear.

Chris: You *are* full of shit.

Ford: I'm old. I have to prove nothing, but remember one thing! I'll never be too old to land you one on the fucking jaw. Are you going to be boring? Christ Walt, you didn't tell me he was boring.

Chris: I'm sorry. I only wish someone would read my script.

Ford: Before the day is out. It is yet morning. What's she like?

Chris: Who?

Ford: You've met her, Walt. What's she like?

Bick: Who?

Ford: The daughter. The daughter of the agency.

Bick: Now don't start nothing, Bill. Please. Don't start nothing.

Ford: I was in hospital once. On the clothes line. Drying out. Once you've accepted it, it's alright, but they smile all the time, and treat every question you ask the way parents treat the child who says 'bugger' the day Granny comes to visit. Don't be suspicious of me. Let me relax. Let me get here. I'm in the greatest city in the world and people want me to write. When a Scottish plumber comes to Paris nobody asks him to plumb. *(Gently)* Now would you both oblige me and have a bloody drink.

Bick: Vodka.

Ford: Rimbaud?

Chris: I don't care. Whisky.

Ford: I've a 12 year old Bell's here. The mid-sixties was a particularly good harvest in Perthshire. It kind of spars with you for six rounds, then knocks you cold. A 'wee goldie' for you, Christopher, and something Russian for you, Walt. *(He pours drinks)* It's a great book, Walt, but we'll kick it when it's down. *(He laughs — then raises his glass)* Here's tae us.

Wha's like us? Damn few an' they're a' dead! *(They drink. Pause)*

Bick: How was New York, Bill?

They sit down, **Ford** *on the sofa.*

Ford: The Jews have moved to the suburbs and the Puerto Ricans have taken over the Bronx. Who moves to the Bronx when the Puerto Ricans start to make it?

Chris: The English.

Ford: Very good, Chris. Very good. Why are we doing it, Walt?

Bick: Huh?

Ford *(holding up the script):* 'The Lord'. Why are we doing it?

Bick: Give us a break, Bill. You wouldn't want me to starve and I can't get into the *new* pictures. I try. I meet the young directors, the young writers. Motor bike pictures. Skinflicks. Iced nipples. Horror. Rock 'n' Roll singers acting Prokoviev.

Ford: I met him.

Bick: Did he strike you as a fag who had a secret desire to be dressed up in Nazi uniform and be whipped by girls with big tits dressed up as the Luftwaffe?

Ford: Can't say as he did, Walt.

Bick: See! I told you, Chris. It's all shit what they're doing now. At least 'The Lord' has a story. I understand that. I can function with that. Does that answer your question, Bill?

Ford: Of course not. Where's Andy?

Bick: He's scouting locations. Spending a fortune in Morocco. How can you spend a fortune in Morocco, for Christ's sakes?

Chris: You can buy shit. Good shit.

Ford: You don't know our Andy. He's strictly a booze man. In the great tradition. Here's to him. *(He drinks)* I had dinner at his house a few months ago, in London. Very movie business. Shepperton. *Bore*ham Wood.

Bick: All British technicians are like Andy.

Ford: Gucci shoes and blazers.

Bick: Right.

Ford: Wanting to live in Beaconsfield or Gerrard Cross to be near the studios which is stupid since the studios are closing down. They live in houses that seem to have been designed by bad art directors. Before dinner you get a goblet, not a glass . . . a kind of silver thing all polished so that the contents taste like a mixture of Johnnie Walker and Duraglit! The dining table is kind of Colonel Saunders Elizabethan like that ridiculous Wimpy Bar at Stratford upon Avon. Swords and guns on the wa' next to a bad portrait of the wife.

Chris: What *do* you like?

Ford: I like Walt. Not sure about you, yet.

Chris: I asked for that.

Ford: Well . . . I like boxing, when it's great. I hate it when it's not. Ali, Pep . . . Willie Pep. Sugar Ray Robinson. I *saw* . . . before your time. I saw Benny Lynch beat Small Montana at Wembley. Great night. Great experience. Like seeing the Mantegna Christ in Milan for the first time or Bogart . . . *arresting* your attention. *He* was a friend. You don't have many o' them by the very nature of . . . well you're looking at a hard friend to put up with, Chris. John Ford. My namesake and I'm sure of his immortality. Balzac of course! The West of Ireland, Suffolk, Scottish football and the Isle of Skye. Scotch whisky always. Pernod and creme de menthe frapee, sometimes . . .

Bick *(nods to* **Chris**)*: He* drinks these things.

Ford: Good. I like the company of women more than most people. I love my grandchildren and don't envy their future. Oh, I don't know. You see, Chris. I don't really hate anybody. Do critics count? Well, I'm a liar. Prizes. I hate prizes. It's hard to write after praise. Prizes make you stop and consider. Energy breakers. There was one I liked, though.

Bick *(sentimental):* We all know what that was Bill.

Ford: Not at all. *That's* the worst prize of all. I mean the David Hay Turnbull Prize. It's for a slim volume of Scottish verse. *Slight pause.*

Chris: Who's David Hay Turnbull?

Ford: He was the bloke that died laughing when he was told that Charles the Second had been restored to the monarchy. Fill us up to him, Chris.
Chris *goes for more drinks.*
Walt *refuses.*

Bick: Charlie's taking us out to lunch.

Ford: Fuck him. I'm going to the races. Longchamps. Coming, Chris.

Chris: I said I'd see Charlie.

Ford: Don't worry about your future so much, Chris. You don't need agents if you've got talent. Is the daughter coming?

Bick: Think so.

Ford: Maybe I could miss the first race.

Bick: Now don't start nothing, Bill. Don't start nothing.

Ford: Who, me?

Bick: Yeah. You. I've seen this guy in action, Chris. 'I'm Bill Ford, who are you?' says he. 'We must have met before'. It's like Ronald Colman. Dated, entirely successful and completely full of shit. Ramon Navarro in a kilt.

Ford: You're lovely, Walt. Thank you for inviting me. We didn't get the cheque and I have, as usual, no readies.

Bick *(gives money):* Here. I got you some English cigarettes.

Ford: Gold Flake. You're a genius, Walt. *(Counts money)* just in case Charlie's daughter would like some champagne between races.

Chris: You're really confident.

Ford *(lighting a cigarette):* Too old to worry about a slap in the face, son. *(Takes a drink)* Thank you. *(Raises the glass)* English measures served here.

Rises, puts some more whisky in the glass and a careful amount of water. Shows it to Chris *on the way back to the sofa.*

In future, Christo*pher. (He drinks)* Where are we meeting?

Bick: They're coming here.

Ford: Good. We don't have to move. Just sit. We three. We could have a 'reading' of Christopher's pages. I could read Joseph, Walt could be Herod.

Walt: Thanks, Bill.

Ford: And you, Chris . . .

Chris: . . . Could be the Virgin Mary. All right. It's the best part, anyway.

Ford: There's not going to be a narrator is there? I can't stand narrators.

Chris: Well, I thought . . .

Ford: Graffiti. I've had one idea, Walt. Glasgow, London, New

York — even Morocco, I dare say . . . filled with graffiti. Political mostly. Let's have '*himself*' pass through graffiti on his donkey.

Bick: That's a great idea, Bill.

Ford: I knew he'd say that, Chris. It's probably a terrible idea. I don't know. Let's do a comedy. The world has seen enough religious movies. It's even been on television. Seven o'clock on a Sunday. Just to keep everyone away from evening service. Ministers and priests and I dare say rabbis, Walt, spouting forth to empty pews and the congregation sitting at home watching Jesus on ATV. The best piece of graffiti ever. Competition. And you've got to play. Chris.

Chris: Belfast. 'Is there a life before death?'

Ford: Knew you'd choose that. Walt?

Bick: I hate your games, Bill.

Ford: Come on, Wal-ter . . .

Bick: Well, it was spooky. In London. Just by the Portobello Road Market. 'Crime is the highest form of sensuality'. Is that okay?

Ford: It's okay, but it's really depressing. Mine was a small town in Scotland. In the Gents. Just above the stall. It read: 'Is *nobody* queer in Kircudbright?' Sad. I pissed myself. I really did.

Chris: Well, you were in the right place to do it.

Ford: Christ! Is *nobody* queer . . .

Bick: Is that the game over?

Ford: Let's read it.

Bick: Look. They're due.

Ford *(with energy and speed):* Are you suggesting that I'm not taking this . . . 'project' . . . as serious as I might. Look, Walt, it's only when we *say* it that we'll know if it's people talking. You know that. I don't know how Jews talk. No offence, Walt. I mean *ancient* Jews, and Romans for Jesus sake. They spoke Latin. We can't have people saying 'sorry buddy. There's no room. This is an Inn not a maternity ward'. But what's the alternative? I know. A narrator. *(American accent)* 'But there was no room at the Inn. So. It came to pass. In a stable. In a manager.' Music swells up here usually and the camera goes all weak at the knees looking at some face lifted film star feeling, *she* thinks, like the paintings the director's forced her to look at for the first time in her life. 'The child was born'. Boom! Boom! Musical climax and cut to three star-gazing ex-marines trying to act wise. It's really hard, Walt. We'll never find out how they *spoke*. Jesus isn't going to be a Swede this time, is he?

Bick: English, we think.

Ford: Shouldn't he be Jewish, Walt?

Bick: He should be cheap. That's the main thing.

Ford: English actors are cheap?

Bick: Yeah.

Chris: That's ridiculous.

Bick: Bullshit! They don't really like movies. They all want to play Shakespeare.

Ford: And so they should. Let's drink to them. I'll have another, Chris.

   Chris *rises.*

Chris: Mr Bickmore?

Ford: Mr Bickmore will have a large vodka.

Bick: I wish you would take a real interest, Bill. Some of it's my own money and things are different nowadays. I'm old fashioned. Out of date. I *will* have vodka.

Ford: Good on you, Walt. Don't you worry, I won't let you down. Promise you.

Bick: Thanks.

Ford: Don't worry. Don't worry. Don't *worry*.
   Slight pause.

Bick: What's the good of composing mazurkas if nobody dances mazurkas no more?

Ford: Have your drink. Pep you up. Thanks, Chris. It must be Matthew's Gospel.

Chris: What makes you say that?

Ford: It's the only one with moral beauty. I was reading it before I passed out on the 'plane. 'Lord have mercy on my son: for he is a lunatick, and sore vexed for oftimes he falleth into the fire and oft into the water'. *(Pause)* Well, that fairly put the tin hat on the conversation. *(Pause)* Bogart. He held court. Aye. Right to the end. Couldn't get down the stairs. Came down in a kind of a . . . dumb waiter, you know? He died cocky somehow. Stylishly. Martini in hand. Chesterfield hanging out of his mouth. Just like in the movies. He coughed. Blood came. Walt was there. Black blood. Bogey turned. He looked Walt right between the eyes . . .

Bick: 'Can't take it, can you?' That's what he said.

Pause. Ford leans against the pillows of the sofa as if to have a nap. Then suddenly:

Ford: Scotland! Pissed out of its mind. Britain, Ireland . . . *(Raises his glass)* THE UNIVERSE! Pissed out of its mind! *(He drinks then leans back on the sofa)*

FADE

SCENE THREE

The suite. Later in the evening. The room is empty. Dark. **Ford** *enters. He turns on the lights. With him,* **Agneta,** *dark, young, Swedish. He moves to the drinks table. She sits down.*

Ford: Brazil is terrific. Oh yes, if you can avoid the poverty and the maimed begging for a copper in the street, Brazil is absolutely terrific. We went with a draft crew. There was this English art director, very talented but very married. We took him to a brothel one night and tried to change that, but we failed miserably. On the way. Well, we weren't exactly making for the brothel, we were headed for a little town called Para*ti* and we drove through the jungle in this rather comfortable car. The horizon was just more jungle and Coca Cola signs. Coca Cola signs are always on the horizon in the Brazilian jungle. Anyway, this fellow. This art director was lonely. That's when I had the idea of the bordello, but really he was lonely for his lady wife who was called Joy or Gay or Mirth or one of those unfortunate English names English parents give to English girls. Anyway, our hero was lonely and

19

he wanted to talk to Laughing Girl. 'In the middle of the jungle?' said Walt, implying that it was impossible. However, there was this assistant called Stuart with us . . . more of him later. He proved to be . . . well . . . ridiculous. Stuart said he could fix up a line from the Jungle to Ladbroke Grove or Camberwell or where-ever this wife was. And he did. My great memory of the art director was astride a telephone pole in the middle of the jungle talking to his wife. All he said was 'How's Julian?' Then he'd pause long enough for Gay to say 'Fine'. 'How's Kimberley?' 'Fine'. So there we were, six grown men on our way to the best Bordello in South America just checking that the art director's children were fine. Then the assistant. Stuart. The young cameraman. Tony. You'll like him. *He* was talking about pop music and Stuart said — he was about forty — 'I was a rock and roll singer once'. Rather sadly. 'Who *were* you?' we asked. 'Never heard of the Landis Brothers?' 'No', came the reply. 'I was Brett Landis', says he. 'Who did you sing?' says I. 'Be Bop a Lula', says he. And he sang it. There we were driving through the jungle, palm trees waving, dusk falling with *the* Brett Landis singing 'Be Bop a Lula'. It was very . . . bizarre. The movies are a rich, crazy, indulgent business but you get to meet people and you're not lonely. What are you going to do when you grow up?

Agneta: Write.

Ford: What if you can't?

Agneta: Get married.

Ford: How did you get involved with Charlie?

Agneta: I'm waiting for a place. Malmo University. Decided to see England. Wrote to an au pair agency. Got the job with Mr Leech.

Ford: It's such an appropriate name for one in his profession.

Agneta: Sorry?

Ford: Oh, nothing. Take your coat off. Drink?

Agneta: Pernod.

Ford: Right. *(He goes to get drinks. Pause)*

Ford: Why are you making me nervous?

Agneta *(smiles):* You know I want to make love to you.

Ford: I'm an old man.

Agneta: Yes.

Pause. He gives drinks.

Ford: They'll be in on us in no time. Charlie and . . . God! . . . Wendy . . .

Agneta: This is a suite. We'll go to your room. You're more smaller than I thought you'd be.

Ford: No.

Agneta: Yes.

Ford: No. Not more smaller. More small. Or just smaller. I'm a wee man.

Agneta: Sorry?

Ford: Oh, drink your Pernod and stop threatening me.

Agneta: Skol!

Ford: Aye, right. *(They drink.)*

Agneta: You expected Caroline, didn't you?

Ford: No. There's lots of things I expected when the agents came, but none of them was Caroline. Oh, you mean Charlie's daughter?

Agneta: Yes. She has large breasts.

Ford: I'm not fussy about large breasts. It's just as well you came instead, isn't it?

Agneta: Sit down. *(He sits down near her.)*

Ford: Why aren't you blonde, Agneta? Swedes are blonde.

Agneta: Caroline's blonde.

Ford: Look. Fuck Caroline.

Agneta: No. I'll fuck you.

Ford: Look, I think you're terrific. I haven't felt the lust I feel at this moment for about twenty years and that's Gospel. Well, ten.

Agneta: Kiss me. *(They kiss. Briefly.)*

Ford: You don't get many points for an ageing writer. This room'll be hoaching with film stars before the month's out. Screwing an ageing writer just makes you seem father fixated and nowadays that's very reactionary.

Agneta: Why are you so strange to me? Here. Alone. You were amazing when you talked to us all in the restaurant. At lunch, then at the racing, then dinner.

Ford: The day must have cost Charlie a fortune.

Agneta: But you had . . . is it called 'grace'?

Ford: No. It's called 'cheek'.

Agneta: I have never wanted to be with anyone so much. I have the pills, don't worry.

Ford: Oh, I'm too old to worry about things like that. Live for the moment, eh?

Agenta: Can I undress?

Ford: How can a girl of . . .?

Agneta: Nineteen. *(She takes off her dress)*

Ford: Turn out the light.

Agneta: Why?

Ford: I'm old. Turn out the light.

She does. Light from the electric fire. She takes the rest of her clothes off and stands, naked. **Ford** *goes over to her. He takes her in his arms, Kisses her, lifting her feet off the ground. He takes her hand. She leads him into the bedroom. The door shuts.*

Pause. The room empty. Long silence.

The main door opens. The light goes on again. **Walt** *comes in with* **Charlie**. *He is English. About fifty, dapper, successful. He still has the trace of his former profession — bad actor.* **Chris** *follows, a bit pissed, with* **Wendy**, *Charlie's wife, blue grey hair, overdressed, nearly fifty.*

Chris *closes the door. They have all had a drink or two.*

Bick *(getting 'nightcaps' as they sit around the room):* The only actor. The only one who did three pictures without a raise in salary, without his agent demanding a bigger caravan, bigger billing, a bigger deal or a piece of the action. The only one and I loved him for it.

Charlie: Who was he, Walt?

Bick: Rin Tin Tin.

They laugh.

(Passing drinks to **Wendy** *and* **Charlie***)* now Charlie, I insist you let me *pay* for . . .

Charlie: My pleasure. So seldom we see you.

Bick: Fifty fifty, whattaya say?

Charlie: My treat. I insist.

Bick *(raising his glass):* Well. Salutay!

Charlie: Oh. Cheers.

They drink. Pause.

Wendy: I thought they'd be back by now. It's late.

Charlie: Don't worry, darling. Agneta's alright.

Bick: Sure she is, Wend. Relax.

Wendy: I know, but . . . you know how it is. I feel responsible. Not to worry.

Slight pause.

Charlie: They probably walked.

Wendy: Of course. She's had a lovely day.

Bick: Yeah. That's it. They walked. Clear night. Stars.

Wendy: I'm silly.

The bedroom door opens. **Ford** *comes into the main room, dressed in a tartan dressing gown. Bare feet. He crosses to the drinks cabinet as if there was no one in the room. He lifts a full bottle of 'Bells' whisky and walks back to the bedroom door. He picks up Agneta's clothes from the floor. He notices everyone and looks* **Wendy** *in the eye as he opens the bedroom door.*

Ford: 'Night. 'Night.

He goes into the bedroom, closing the door behind him. The room is full of stunned people.

Long silence.

Then **Chris** *can can be heard laughing. He goes through the first and second stages of laughter very quickly, and finally is laughing at himself laughing. Eventually the faces around him force him to stop. He does. Starts again, briefly. Then stops. He puts on a frown.*

Chris: Excuse me. *(He goes to his room)*

Pause.

Wendy: Charlie?

Charlie: Yes?

Wendy: That could be Caroline in there. Do you realize what is happening? Do you realize what is taking place. If *you* don't—

Charlie: It isn't Caroline, darling.

Wendy: But it's happening *here*. It doesn't matter who it is. You're responsible. They are next door and you . . . you're quite content to sit here having a 'nightcap', as you call it, while your staff are being *raped*. She's almost *family*.

Bick: Don't get upset, Wend.

Wendy: Upset!

Charlie: Wendy, be quiet. You never understood artists.

Wendy: The police. I'll ring the police.

Bick: The kid knows what she's doin'. She's twenty-one and kids nowadays . . .

Wendy: She is *not* twenty-one. She is nineteen and I'm her guardian. You men!

She rises. **Chris** *returns.*

Chris: How's everyone's drink?

Wendy *(to* **Charlie**): Do you know what he's doing to that girl?

Charlie: I don't hear any complaints.

Wendy: You're as bad as the rest. Trips abroad. You forget. All of you have responsibilities. This is what you get up to. Cannes. Tehran. Hotel rooms. No wonder the business is in the state that it's in. You've only yourselves to blame. Behaving like adolescents. Children. When are you going to grow up? I'm helpless. What am I supposed to do?

Charlie: You're supposed to do nothing. Don't cause a scene . . .

Bick: Yeah. Don't get hysterical, Wend. There'll be a happy ending.

Charlie: Chris has just asked you if you'd like another drink.

Wendy: No, thank you very much. Walter, could you call a taxi?

Charlie: I'm staying. For a while.

Wendy: You are *not* staying. Walter is going to call a taxi and we are going back to the hotel. We are going back and we are going back to London on the first flight possible out of here and we are taking that girl who is through there with that . . . peasant . . . home with us and she in turn is going to pack her bags and get the first flight back to her own people in Sweden. That is what you are going to do . . .

Bick: I'll call a cab.

Chris: It's been an amazing day. *(Slight pause)* One way and another.

Wendy: Charlie?

Charlie: Yes, Wendy.

Wendy: Have you been unfaithful to me?

Chris: Christ!

Wendy: Have you?

Bick: Wend. Don't start nothing.

Wendy: I am asking my husband a question. It may be important that there are witnesses present.

Bick: God!

Wendy: Well?

Bick: Look, Charlie. You'll get a cab in the lobby. Maybe you'd better . . . well . . . look . . . I'll see the kid alright.

Wendy: I'm waiting. I want to know.
Slight pause.

Charlie: No.

Wendy: Do you *swear?*

Chris: I think I'm pissed.

Charlie: This is *quite* embarrassing.

Wendy: Swear. Is there a Bible?

Chris: The room's full of Bibles, Wendy. King James. New English. Mormon. The lot! Take your pick.

Charlie: I will not swear.

Wendy: So you're as bad. Filth. He's nothing. He's just a peasant. Nobody's ever finished any of his boring old books anyway. He came from nothing. No backbone. No class. A peasant. Pure and simple.

Chris *(angry):* Wendy, can I say something?

Bick: You're drunk, kid. Turn in. Okay?

Chris: Walt. Don't feel responsible. Pretty sound proof, the Georges Cinq, don't you think? No, I'm serious, Walt. What have *they got to do with you?* (Pointing at **Wendy**) Fuck her. That's what I think if anybody wants to hear an honest opinion. Jealousy will get you nowhere, Wendy, my darling. I was just . . . yes, what was I going to remark . . . yes, I was just going to remark that I've never ever met anybody quite like you before, Wendy . . . except my mother and it might surprise you to know that I *hated* my mother. That's all.
Pause. **Wendy** *sits.*

Bick: Just get in the cab. Please.

Charlie: Goodnight, darling.

Wendy: I'm not moving from this chair without some kind of . . . conclusion or decision or action or something from you.

Chris: There's plenty of room . . .

Bick: Shut up kid, hear?

Wendy: You're all *infected.* You envy him. Carrying on like a twenty-year old undergraduate when he's old enough to be a grandfather. . . .

Charlie: He is a grandfather, Wendy.

Wendy: You're very brave suddenly, Charlie Leech, and old! 'Where have the good times gone? Why can't I live without standards, morals . . . the jungle?' Maybe it's this city that does it to you.

Charlie: Well, it certainly doesn't do it to you.

Wendy: Expense accounts . . . loose living . . .

Bick *(drink talking a bit):* Will you . . . will you *all* . . . just SHUT THE FUCK UP! This is my suite. I pay to stay here and I can pay for who I like to stay here with me. I can have people thrown down the stairs who are unwelcome guests in my suite and I can give hospitality and drink and friendship to any person I want because this is a free country. I am a free man and this is my suite. So just . . . *blow,* will ya? Vamoose. Scram. Charlie, I'd be eternally grateful if you'd just take that woman . . . take her downstairs and in the lobby ask anyone in uniform to get you a cab and put it on my bill. I have chosen to pay for a cab to take you and your wife to *your* suite where you can invite who you like to share and recreate themselves but this is *my* suite and I want you both *out!* Is that clear? A friend. A dear friend of mine is balling a very attractive, interesting, open, bright, unsophisticated, unboring, unEnglish young lady in my suite and the best of luck to him. My other friend . . . Less close, but equally welcome is getting stoned on my scotch in my suite, and the best of luck to him, too. I've given these two friends of mine a grand time and in my business there haven't been too many grand times lately, at least not for those of us who've grown old in this business and if I may be personal, I haven't enjoyed myself so much in years. That girl in there, oh, Wendy, baby, she's the one with the class, *you're* like me, you're the one with the experience and nobody needs that. Now will you please in the silence after I've shut my mouth . . . go.

Silence. They go. **Charlie** *makes an apologetic gesture. Pause.* **Chris** *brings a drink to* **Walt.**

Chris *sits, drinking.*
Chris: Well done, Walt.
Bick: Thank Christ it *wasn't* Caroline.

FADE

SCENE FOUR

The suite. Early next morning.

Ford *sits in his dressing gown on the sofa, a brandy in his hand.*
Agneta *sits on the carpet, leaning against his legs. She wears his Union shirt.*

Ford: I have nothing to leave. There is no legacy. Nothing said .
. . *exactly.* Do you know? . . . on the Isle of Rhum . . .
Agneta: Rum?
Ford: Yes. R.H.U.M. In the Inner Hebrides. In Scotland . . . on
the Isle of Rhum there are golden eagles. They may be the
last golden eagles because they have something to live on.
Deer. The eagles swoops down on the herd and picks the
youngest, weakest calf . . . attacks . . . and feeds . . . well on
the calf. But once I saw a stag . . . his doe was screaming in a
pain beyond anything I had heard before . . . that scream . . .
and the eagle was still devouring her child. The stag . . .
snorted . . . threw his head in the air . . . in anger, but in
pride . . . like a king in the jungle . . . on the island the stag
has to be king and other stags and does are looking to him for
rule. He runs — faster than you would imagine he'd go —
chasing the eagle. But the eagle doesn't fly away. He is heavy
with the young deer, so the stag ate him — whole. And in
winter the hare and the fox turn white. Blend with the
snowfall. It sounds like magic but it's nature. I saw that. And
I saw the eagle eaten . . . alive, and it didn't *change* me. I
wrote what I was going to write — finished what I had

started. I may as well never have seen a stag kill a golden eagle on Rhum. A special thing was shown to me. I'm supposed to have been born with eyes to see *that* — tell *that* . . . true, but I carried on writing whatever it was. Inventing. Telling the story of my Township, my people, my *invented* county, my invented county that made me famous. Isn't that — a kind of . . . lying?

Agneta: You've told it to me. You can still write it.

Ford: I've forgotten what is feels like.

Agneta: I'll get dressed.

Ford: No. I like it in the morning.

Agneta: I've made you trouble.

Ford: My dear, there's trouble, and trouble. You've made trouble for Walt. How he got shot of Wendy beats me. Och, he's prepared for all eventualities, our Walt.

Agneta: He's nice.

Ford: That's *his* trouble. It doesn't agree with a man like Walt, niceness. He's made a lot of money, but he doesn't have the spark, the risk it takes to really crack his game. He employs burnt out, written out, petered out old farts like me. And shagged out if you had anything to do with it.

Agneta: Sorry?

Ford: Oh, give us a kiss. *(They kiss)* Will you write me letters? From Sweden?

Agneta: If you want. Maybe it's better to finish. Done.

Ford: You're hard.

Agneta: Old married men can hurt me.

Ford: Oh, don't worry about Sarah. She's a rock, poor Sarah, but don't worry, I'll tell her. It's odd. She was always called 'poor Sarah'. No, but write.

Agneta: Why?

Ford: Selfish, maybe. It's all I can write now, is letters. I write good letters. I think someday they'll collect them in a book and you'll be a good fuck on the long road to literary history. Sorry.

Agneta: There's worse than you.

Ford: If you think I was lookin' for a compliment, you'd be right. Christ, you're A.I. plus Agneta, know that?

Agneta: A.I. plus?

Ford: Aye. Ten outa ten. Top marks. All departments. Kosher. Hot stuff. First division. Class by yersel' . . . *Ace.*

Agneta: Thank you. I think I'd better get some clothes on . . .

Ford: You're fine in that shirt. Never suited me.

Agneta: But — Walt and Christopher . . .

Ford: I wish you could do something about Christopher. Give *him* one. Cheer 'im up.

Agneta: I don't like young men.

Ford: Thank Christ. Listen, you're one in a million.

Agneta: Drink?

Ford: No, it's six o'clock in the morning. I can last till seven . . . usually. This is just a . . . it's a word I invented. A 'morningcap'. I know it's wasted on you. I wish I knew some jokes in Swedish. But write me letters. No one writes letters anymore. Don't phone me. I don't answer the phone. I pretend I'm working. But I'm just sitting there in my room looking down at the water and the cranes and the shipyard and the grey. Just sitting. Writing sometimes, but only letters or . . . patching up for Walt. Elastoplasting some rubbish and putting my name to it.
Slight pause.

Agneta *(kissing him on the forehead):* Thank you.

    Agneta *moves to the bedroom door. She turns.*

Ford: Aye. Just give us a minute to collect mysel'.
She goes in. Ford sits.

After a pause, **Ford** *rises to follow her.* **Bickmore** *enters. He is dressed in a silk polka dot dressing gown over his pyjamas.*

Ford: How ye?

Bick: Hi.

Ford: You look less than well, Walt. Can I switch you an egg? Switched egg and milk, that's the . . .

Bick: No. It's very kind, but no.

Ford: Do you good. Honest.

Bick: Look, I don't want a fuckin' egg. You mother, whattaya mean by . . .?

Ford: Temper. Wal-ter . . .

Bick: Christ, Bill. Why do you — do it?

Ford: Well. Honest answer. When I have one whisky, I feel bigger . . . wiser . . . taller. When I have a second I feel superlative. When I have more There's no holding me.

Bick: But we're supposed to be . . .

Ford: We *are* friends, Walt.

Bick: Thanks, Buddy. Gee, thanks. Wendy's out of box. Bananas!

Ford: You're so modern, Walt. How you manage to keep up with the parlance of the day never ceases to astonish me. Send her a bunch of flowers.

Bick: Yeah, that's right. First thing. Look, there I go again. Cleaning up after you. Trying to be nice, keep the peace, smooth everything over. I don't like Wendy Leech. Why should I send her flowers? You send her flowers.

Ford: I don't want to send her flowers. I can't stand her.

Bick: But you never know when . . .

Ford: Walt. I know you're getting old, but you're never going to be old enough or past it enough to need Charlie Leech. Never.

Bick: Guess we shouldn't send flowers.

Ford: See how you feel in the morning. *(Slight pause)* Look, I'm sorry if I caused you any embarrassment. Won't happen again.

Bick: You mean you're quitting?

Ford: Certainly not. I'm having a wonderful time. I'm eternally grateful.

Bick: I only have hangovers when I'm with you. I only have colitis when I'm with you. You know that?

Ford: *Sure* you wouldn't like a . . . .?

Bick: Look, I don't want a boiled egg, a poached egg, a fried egg, a coddled egg, a switched egg, or Eggs Benedict . . . alright?

Ford: Please yourself.'Night, 'Night. *(Turns to go into bedroom.)*

Bick: Bill?

Ford: Aye?

Bick: What's to happen?

Ford: I'm trying, Walt. Thinking about it. Honest. Trying to help. Do you want me to go?

Bick: Let's talk in the morning.

Ford: It's morning now, Walt. *(Takes his pocket watch out of his dressing gown)* Six o'clock. We're ahead of the world. Nobody's up yet.

Bick: Oh yes, they are.

Ford: Aye. No doubt it's lunchtime in Hollywood and cocktails in New York and people are sitting by the pool. Making deals. And all your friends are shouting down the phone. Maybe they're talking about you, Walt. You think they are anyway, so what does it matter if they're not. They're having screenings, buying novels and turning them into properties. No story's as good as the one the other fella has bought, is it, Walt? They're flying across the American continent as if it was gallant little Belgium. And here you are. Away from that. It's raining outside and you can't really function away from the sun, can you? Here you are, with me, an old pissartist, making another Jesus picture. Christ, man, you're worth the whole fuckin' lot of them. There's got to be more than *that*, Walt. What's left is us? Eh?

> **Walt** *goes to the window.*

Bick: How did you know it was raining?

Ford: I had the fire department set it up. It's not real rain. If you don't like it, turn it off. You're payin' for it.

Bick: It's so quiet. Out there. That new glass stops the noise of the cars. We could be anywhere.

Ford: Any hotel suite could be anywhere.

> **Ford** *goes to the drinks cabinet for the least sensation of cognac. Pause.*

Bick: Howard Hughes is gone. Another dead pirate. I'm keeping you. I only came in for the Alka Seltzer. In my case.

Ford: Oh, sit yourself down, Walt. The young 'uns have their whole life in front of them. Surely two old men can sit down and talk about the wee bit of the future that's theirs. She'll be asleep.

Bick: I like her. That's why I blew up at Wendy.

Ford: You're not like the others, Walt. You never had to pay for it.

Bick: I will not drink again. I will not drink again. Dear Lord, I will not drink again.

Ford: Mind over matter. Hangovers. Mind over matter.

Bick: You just don't stop drinking long enough. If you did, your hangover would be so big it'd kill ya.

Ford: What an epitaph. Died of massive hangover. Left his liver to science.

Bick: Gonna start layin' off? What about it?

Ford: Sure. Tomorrow.

Bick: I would consider it a large personal favour. . . .

Ford: Oh, don't beg, Walt. It doesnae suit ye.

Bick: Look, you motherfucker. You got a God-given talent. Nobody writes like you and you damn well know it. Just . . . write, will ya? I don't care if it's for me. Come March my accountants will probably find a way to make you tax deductable, but just write. Your novel. Anything. Just *you* function.

Ford: That's what I'm here for, Walt. Had my fun. Well. Will have by breakfast.

Bick: You're my only writer who never listened to me. I've had guys — well, most of them were so bad they shouldn't have been left alone in a room with a typewriter.

Ford: Very good, Walt. Very good.

Slight pause.

Bick: I got the blues.

Slight pause.

Ford: Can I be honest with you?

Bick: Hey, wait a minute. You don't have the big C, do ya?

Ford: Don't be so melodramatic, Walt. Of course, I haven't got the . . . Cancer. Christ, you're cheery.

Bick: Well, what the fuck *is* wrong with ya?

Ford: Edward G. Robinson.

Bick: What?

Ford: Eddie Robinson. He'd be very good. Good actor. Eddie Robinson. Three of the best paintings I ever saw were in his house. Cezanne's the best.

Bick: Look, I know it's six in the morning, an' I know you think my brain's by the pool on the telephone, but what the fuck are you talking about?

Ford: But he's dead. Died. Not long ago, was it?

Bick: Who is dead, Bill?

Ford: Edward G. Robinson!

Bick: They're all dead. Bogart. Robinson. Gable. Tracy. They're all dead.

Ford: But that's the point. You see, Walt. You're the old movies. There's a sense of history about you. Soon you'll *all* be dead and no one will be able to see what you were like. The movies will survive you, but you could show them how you *make* the movies, fuckups and all. Drunk writers, agents' wives, for Christ's sake, nymphette au pair girls in their beds. Directors who had to toe the line. You could show them how many films you fucked up, Walt and how you fucked them up. How many writers you drove to the drink. Oh, I don't mean me, but don't you see it? You don't, do you? Now that Robinson's dead who'd we get to play it?

Bick: What? To play what?

Ford: You, Walt. You. Sean Connery can play me. I always wanted to be tall. To be thought of as tall. My face looks like the face of a tall man. You know? On the book jacket.

Bick: Okay, Bill. We've got Connery. We've got . . . Steve McQueen.

Ford: Is that your fantasy? Steve McQueen. You disappoint me, Walt. All of a sudden, you disappoint me.

Bick: Look, I'm tired. I'm hungover and I'm tired. Just cry off sick and no hard feelings. Okay?

Ford *(passionately):* What do you know about . . . a carpenter, Walt. A carpenter. A man that works with his hands. What does Chris know about a fuckin' carpenter, come to that. Sweet Fanny Adams. What did you know about Brazil? Oh, aye. You knew the currency was soft, but you didn't know the government was hard till half the crew ended up in the jail. Before you're *too* old, make something you *know*. The movies are your life. You walk down the street and we know who you are, what you are. You're nearly a cliché, for Christ's sake!

Bick: Hey, wait a min . . .

Ford: You bloody well are. Use it. Stop farting about with Jesus. 'The Lord'. Show them us making the Lord.

Bick: An eight million dollar documentary? You must be out of your mind. What would New York say?

Ford: Fuck New York.

Bick: Easy for you.

Ford: Look this is no documentary wi' wobbly cameramen following us around like detectives in a divorce case. This is classical. Accurate. I promise I'll help ye, Walt. Promise. Go off the juice. Maybe. Well, tail off any rate. If I could have got you into a book, Walt . . . But, by Christ I'll nail ye once an' for all and Steve McQueen better get it *right*. . . .

Bick: Who wants to see a movie about movies?

Ford: Me. It's about time we stopped tryin' to please everybody and tried to please ourselves.

Bick *(grins):* It'll be more like a war movie.

Ford: *Ab*solutely.

Bick: But it'll be . . . who's gonna direct it?

Ford: That's never worried you up to now, Walt. Look, if the script's right a fuckin' robot can direct a movie. You buy 'im up an' I'll flatter 'im round. This prize o' mine comes in bloody handy at times.

Bick: You're a bastard. It'll be so bad. People will be advised to stay away from the neighbourhood in case it comes on rain and they have to go into the theatre for shelter, it'll be so bad.

Ford: But what if it's *true*. I've seen you nearly break your heart. Yes. Wake up Chris? What do ye say? (**Ford** *moves to* **Chris's** *bedroom door. He bangs hard*) Reveille, Chris. Hands off your cocks. Pull up your socks!

> **Ford's** *bedroom door opens.* **Agneta** *enters*

Christ. Did I wake ye, hen?

Agneta: Come to bed. It's late.

Ford: Early.

Agneta: I'm home tomorrow . . . today.

> *He goes over to her, kisses her briefly.*

Ford *(leading her to the sofa. In a hurry):* Sit down. Beside Walt. I love ye, I love ye. Honest.

Agneta *(sitting down):* Walter. I am loved by an amazing old man.

Ford: Enough of the old. Just watch it. There's Chris.

> **Chris** *comes in.*

How ye?

Chris: Oh . . . Oh . . . God, never again. *(He groans)*

Bick: Hangover?

Chris: My tongue's . . . growing.

Ford: A switched egg. Just haud on a minute Want tae talk to ye. Don't worry. Switched egg and milk'll do the trick or . . . a hair of the dog?

Chris: Thank you. No.

Ford: Gentlemen *be* seated!

Bick: It's back to analysis for me. And this time it's going to cost me a fortune.

Ford: Oh. Optimism, Walt. *(Quickly)* Look. Listen, start at the beginning. My book's called 'A Country Tale' and it's no good, right? That's first. Oh, I'll finish it sometime and they'll publish it, and my loyal critics will be loyal and the old enemies like that Lesbian whoor in Edinburgh will libel me. But that won't make it any good, either.

Bick: Look, we're all broke up about your book, just. . . .

Chris: Can I read it?

Ford: No.

Chris: Why not?

Ford: 'Cause you'll be the one that's read it. That's why. 'I liked it . . . in parts . . . but he didn't live up to his early promise. Can this be from the same author who gave us . . .' forgetting you'll never write one *sentence* in the same league. Sorry. That was unkind.

Chris: At least I really know what you really think.

Ford: Oh, Chris. Fuck. Wait a minute. I propose . . . I've had this. Well, I don't think there's any point in fartin' around with . . . trying to make Jews talk and Romans talk and. . . . Oh, Christ, tell 'im, Walt.

Bick: Chris.

Chris: What's going on? Am I fired?

Ford: You see, Walt. He doesn't know how interesting he is, either.

Bick: Bill wants us to make the movie about us making the movie, but I think I'm right here, but Chris, I'm against it. Well, we make the movie also, but every time the audience settle into it — you know . . . well these . . . well it's the Sermon on the Mount, right?

Chris: Yeah?

Bick: And after he's done a bit of it and the crowd have done their reaction shots and he speaks a bit more, the truck arrives with lunch and you see that I'm there and. . . .

Ford: That's a bit obvious, Walt, but that's what I mean. And Walt is the star. Played by Steve McQueen.

Chris: George Burns.

Bick: George Burns is nearly two hundred years old.

Ford: But would you believe it?

Chris: They would if it was true.

Ford: When's that actor coming?

Bick: Who?

Ford: Charlie's client. The unknown.

Chris: He's not *unknown!*

Bick: Tomorrow. Rinzler.

Chris: Ralph Rinzler.

Ford: He's coming to meet us to talk about Jesus.

Chris: He's very good.

Ford: But even if he's terrible. Even if he doesn't get the part, he might get in the . . . movie. You see? He might be the guy who *didn't* get the part. He's probably a damn sight more gifted than the one who does. We make things happen like seeing him, interviewing him, and then we make our script, and then we make our movie.

Bick: Won't make a dime. Not a plug nickel.

Chris: There were three abortions on the last film I wrote.

Ford: But there was nothing as exciting in the script.

Chris: Thanks.

Agneta: I'm tired. Really.

Ford: Sorry, love. Maybe the Virgin Mary'll get off wi' a wise man an' St Matthew'll be shackin' up wi' Joseph of Arimathea.

Bick: Yeah. That's what scares the hell outa me. Okay. Let's all turn in. Again. Show me a script. I can't get a hot director without a script. Without a hot director, I can't get a deal. It's hard times.

Ford: Steve McQueen. Jesus!

Chris: That cure you were talking about. . . .

Bick: Chris. Take my advice. Don't have a switched egg.

Ford: We must. Hold on, Agneta. Five minutes. The last today. As they used to *do* in Fontain*bleu.* Claret for ladies. Burgundy for gentlemen and brandy for heroes. Will you have a wee cognac, Walt?

ACT TWO

SCENE ONE

The suite. Late afternoon of the same day.

The arrangement of the furniture has changed. The sofa is no longer centre. More space. Less cosy. More like a place of work. A storyboard leaning from the top of the sideboard. On it, sketches from the art director and photographs of Morocco. The second table is littered with books of paintings and photos of actors.

A knock on the main door, not loud. Chris *moves towards it. . .* Bickmore *sits at a table pretending to look through photographs.* Ford *pours another drink.*

The main door opens. There is no one there. Then, the pitter-pat of rushed footsteps up the hotel corridor. Looking as if he's 'goofed' Ralph Rinzler *finally appears in the doorway. He is in his twenties. An actor. He wears a velvet suit over a Russian peasant shirt. He is dark, growing a beard in order to look like* 'The Lord'. *His hair is too long to suit him. This is also an attempt at the El Greco's. But,* Ralph *is a good actor and knows how important this role could be to his career. Charlie has told him and has probably described the two strangers he is about to meet.*

Ralph: Sorry. I thought. . . . Wrong door. . . . I wasn't sure about the main. . . . Sorry I'm a bit late. . . .
Chris: Ralph, can I introduce. . . .?
Bick *(rising):* Walter F. Bickmore.

Ralph: Came to the right door first then. . . . Ralph. *(shaking hands)* Ralph Rinzler.

Ford: You could sing that if you had an air to it.

Chris: And can I introduce. . . .?

Bick: Saw you, Ralphy. Interesting play.

Ralph: We heard you were in. It was a bit 'second nightish' that night.

Ford: Bill Ford, son. *(shakes hands)* Drinky pinky?

Ralph: Well. . . .

Bick: You were good. Damn good.

Ralph: Good part. You can't do much. . . .

Ford: No. You certainly can't do that.

Ralph: Honoured to meet you . . . Mr Ford. I've read 'The. . . .

Ford: Hope we're payin' your fares. Hotels. Anything you spend claim! Walt's made o' money.

     Ralph *laughs nervously.*

Relax. We're only seeing about three hundred and twenty nine other blokes.

Bick: Yeah. Relax. Just want you to read a bit for. . . .

Ralph: Wasn't sure whether I'd have to . . . sometimes they . . . I haven't prepared . . . Charlie. . . .

Ford: Fuck Charlie. . . .

Chris *(assertive):* Does anyone else get a chance to speak? Eh?

     Slight pause.

Ford: The floor is yours.

Chris: Could you tell us, Ral . . . what it would mean . . . you know . . . getting the part?

Ralph: Well, I'd no longer be 'Time Out's' favourite actor.

Bick: What's 'Time Out'?

Chris: It's a magazine, Walt. In London.

Bick: Oh. You married?

Ralph: No.

Ford: Shacking up with anybody?

Ralph: Well . . .

Ford: Be yourself, son. We want an actor no' a virgin. You grew a beard. Now that's interesting. The power you have, Walt. Ralph grew a beard. Didn't you, Ralph? If it had been 'The King and I' he'd a' shaved his hair off.

Ralph: Well. . . .

Ford: Acting's a mug's game. Too much. . . . Humiliation. Too much . . . bravery required.

Bick: The way we see the part, Ralphy. Tell ya straight. Young Aggressive. Ballsy. He's a revolutionary, right? Violent. Takes the Peasants by the scruff of the neck an' says 'Fuck those Roman bastards. This is Israel. This is our promised land'.

Ford: Don't recall these lines in the "Lamb's Book of Life', Walt. Look, we don't know what we're doin' son. You come highly recommended. Chris here thinks you're ace, but I want to know about . . . *you,* you know? What do you do when you . . . well, when you're not . . . acting . . . what's it called?

Ralph: Signing on?

Ford: Aye. Spade a spade. When you're on the dole.

Ralph: Hope my lady's working.

Ford: She's an actress?

Ralph: Yeah.

Ford: Would you go to bed wi' Walt to get the part?

Bick: Jesus Christ!

Ford: Aye. That's the part.

Ralph: *No way!*

Ford: Are *ye* sure?

Ralph: Are you drunk?

Ford: Don't come the bully wi' me, son. Just answer the question.

Chris *(to Ford):* Get off his back, eh?

Ralph: Look, I don't know if I want the part. My agent says fly to Paris. See them. I fly to Paris.

Ford: So Charlie runs your life?

Ralph: Charlie doesn't run my life. Even if I got the part the compromise. . . .

Ford: What compromise? This film is going to be directed by the D. W. Griffith of tomorrow. Every frame a Rembrandt.

Ralph: Who *is* directing it?

Chris: We don't know.

Bick: I'm in the middle of very serious discussions with Milos Forman.

39

Ralph: Marvellous.

Ford: *How* d'ye *know?*

Chris *(to* **Ford***):* You've *got* the part, O.K.?

Bick: Christopher. . . .

Ford: Leave 'im be, Walt. . . .

Chris: Try it on one of the other. . . .

Ford: Three hunner an' twenty nine? Right! Sorry . . . eh . . . Ralph. All will be revealed, I hope tae Christ, at a later date.

Ralph: Are you writing a book?

Ford: No. I'm . . . resting.

Ralph *(smiling at that):* I will have a drink.

Ford: Help yourself.

Ralph: Thanks.

> *He rises and goes to drinks table.*

Chris: I'll get it. G and T?

Ralph: Thanks.

> **Chris** *pours the gin and tonic.* **Ralph** *is standing. Uncomfortable silence. Then* **Ralph** *notices the photographs on the board.*

Ralph: Is that the location?

Ford: This is the location.

Bick: Yeah. We're going to Morocco. Hasn't changed since. . . .

Chris: One gin and tonic.

Ralph: Thanks, Chris. *(He sits)*

Ford: What did you mean by compromise?

Ralph: Sorry?

Ford: What compromise? Come on.

Ralph: Oh . . . I don't know. There's been lots of films about . . . Who made his name? Whatever happened to Jeffrey Hunter?

Bick: He died.

Ralph: Oh. Well, the others then. Maybe it's impossible.

Bick: There's never been a good script. We got a great script. It's gonna be a great movie, Ralphy. It's got a story. An unforgettable story. The greatest story ever told. It could make you, kid. Two things gotta like you; the camera and the public. They like ya, you're made. The rest is publicity.

Ford: What would you be doin' if Walt here gie's ye the bum's rush?

Ralph: Eh? Oh . . . they've offered Orlando, Orsino and Tybalt at . . .

Bick: Look, kid. This is the lead, right. That picture you gotta share.

Chris: It isn't a picture, Walt.

Bick: What the hell is it, then?

Chris: Shakespeare.

Bick: Shakespeare. Whoever made a dollar acting Shakespeare? How much are they payin' ya, kid? Two hundred dollars a week? Three hundred?

Ralph: Look, I'm not at all that interested in money.

Ford: Christ. An artist. Or a liar.

Bick: English actors are crazy.

Ralph: He's a good director.

Bick: Directors. Listen, Ralphy, can I tell you the facts of life? God-*dammit,* I hire the director an' if he doesn't work out, I fire the director. How many directors are there in England? In Hollywood? Directors are a dime a dozen. Have you ever heard of a director hiring a producer or firing a producer, huh?

Ralph: Well. No.

Bick: Right. God-dammit, kid, you're about to be invented. Like one day a guy said 'Let's put a stripe in the toothpaste'. He's never looked back an' because we believed him, we think we're walkin' around with fewer cavities, less decay. We believed in him. Same thing here. I say Ralph Rinzler over an' over . . . 'Ralph Rinzler' . . . 'Ralph Rinzler' . . . 'Zat your real name?

Ralph: Well, no. Feinmesser. Reuben Feinmesser.

Bick: Charlie's pretty smart. So . . . 'Ralph Rinzler' . . . 'Ralph Rinzler'. . . .

Ford: I think we've got the point, Walt.

Bick: And before long you're . . . invented like . . . Coca Cola or Marilyn *Mon*roe . . . poor baby.

Ralph: Did you *know* Marilyn Mon*roe*?

Bick: She drove in my car. . . .

Ford *(to* **Chris***):* He's off.

Bick: In the Hollywood hills. I took her back from a party at Cukor's house. It was late an' . . . well she just wanted to drive, I guess. It was raining. Not a downpour, just spots o' rain. She wouldn't let me put the hood up. She said 'Stop round the corner'. Well, I thought . . . what's she want screwin' me — in the back of the car — in the rain? The party was full o' handsome guys. But nothing happened. I stopped the car. The rain was getting pretty heavy now. She got out. She walked along the beam of my car lights . . . stood there. She could always find her light. She pulled her dress off. She had nothin' on underneath. She stretched out her arms, looked up to the sky . . . and was . . . washed . . . dancing in the rain. I just . . . came.

      Pause.

Ford: Well, Ralph. Follow that.

Bick: Give me a drink, Chris.

Chris: Sure.

      Chris *pours a vodka tonic for* **Walt.**

Ralph: I don't think I want to be . . . 'invented'.

Bick: Ya crazy?

Chris: Can I speak?

Bick: I like the cut of you, Ralphy. I want you to know that.

Ralph: Thank. . . .

Ford: Have you ever seen somebody *make* something, son?

Ralph: I've seen my father make a shoe. Gave up in the end. Making. Couldn't compete with mass. . . .

Ford: Same's happening to the weavers in Lewis. You're lookin' at one of the last Harris Tweed jackets. But we're gonnae show folk how you make a movie.

Ralph: You could tell a good shoe by wearing it. How do you wear a movie?

Ford: Clever cunt.

Bick: I wish the kid would read the script. Anything. Just act. Give him some to read. Anything.

Chris *(meaning/*Ford*)*: Only if *he* stops being such a drag . . .

Ford: There are too many people. Well, there's Saint Matthew for a start, an' there's you, Walt, an' me and Chris an' the director, whoever he is. . . .

Chris: Maybe it should be Orson Welles.

Ford: Aye. Look what happened to him. Advertising the best beer in the world. Christ, Walt. What have folk like you done tae folk like me?

Bick: Is it my fault when you don't learn the business? Why is everyone trying to lay it at me? What have I done? I don't even *know* Orson Welles. Lives in Europe somewhere. Goes to bullfights. I hate bullfights.

Ford: That's it. It's an industry. It isn't a trade.

> *Pause.*

Most piano tuners are blind. Know that? Stands to reason.

> *Slight pause.*

Hey, Chris. Gie 'im this to read.

> *He lifts a book from the desk and hands it with the place marked to* **Ralph.**

Could you read that for us, son?

Ralph: Oh. Yes, we did it at drama school. . . .

Bick: What the hell is it?

Ford: Wait an' see, Walt. Surprise, surprise.

Ralph: Could I have a little time to . . .

Bick: Long as you want, kid. Just take your time. What the hell is it?

Ford: We're trying to find out how Jews talk, Walt.

Bick: I know how Jews talk. I know how Jews *Talk.*

Ralph: Yeah.

Ford: Just listen.

Ralph: Shall I stand up?

> *Pause.*

Ford: No, sit where ye. . . .

Bick: Yeah, stand up.

Ford: Stand up. Ready when you are.

Bick: Thank you, Ralphy.

Ralph: *(reading):*
With bittirfull bale have I bought,
Thus, man, all thi misse for to mende.
On me for to looke lette thou noght,
How baynly my body I bende.
No wighte in this worlde wolde have wende
What sorrowe I suffre for thy sake.
Manne, kaste the thy kyndnesse be kende,
Trewe tente un-to me that thou take,
    And treste.

For foxis ther dennys have thei
Birdis hase their nestis to paye,
But the sone of man this daye
    Hase noght on his head for to reste.
        Slight pause.

Ford: Very good.

Chris: Amazing, isn't it?

Bick: Yeah. Now what the fuck was it? Was it scotch?

Ford: No, English. It was done by butchers and poulterers in well . . . fourteen somethin'. . . .

Bick: Are you guys suggesting . . .

Ford: We're suggesting nothing, Walt. But you listened.

Bick: Sure I listened. The boy's come all the way from London, England. He comes recommended. I paid his fare. I'll be getting the bill from the Plaza. Sure I listened, but they've walked out in Dayton, Ohio, and the word has spread that the movie is a bomb. Look, Ralphy, boy, we'll get ourselves organized, send you a script an' you can test. How's that? We'll test you saying somethin' in English when these two mothers stop fucking around.

Ford: I'm glad we heard it. Thanks, Ralph.

Bick: People think I don't know what's going on, but I know what's going on.

The telephone rings.

Ford: Nothin's goin' on, Walt. Well, if that's it for the day, I'm off tae 'Patrick's', then the 'Rotonde', then the 'Chapelain'. Said I'd meet the wee girl in that vicinity. Comin' for a cafe crawl, Chris?

Chris *has gone to the telephone.*

Chris: It's for you, Mr Bickmore. Your wife.

Ford: Rachel. We'll be here a' day.

Walt *goes to the phone.*

Bick: Hi, hi, Rachel. Fine. Fine. Yes, he's fine. How's . . .? Good. They're fine.

Ford *(goes to the main door):* Paris this way.

Chris *and* **Ralph** *rise to leave.*

Bick: Hey, wait a *minute!* Rachel . . . I was . . . We're really deep in conference . . .

Ford: A bientôt, Walt.

Walt *waves.* **Ford** *closes the door as he follows* **Ralph** *and* **Chris** *out.*

Occasionally during the following speech, the distant sound of a demonstration is heard from the street below. Sirens blaring. Tear gas.

Bick: You want what sent? A hat. Sure. You've got it there. It's in Vogue Magazine, September 1974? Well, how do you expect me to . . .? Try? Sure, I'll try. Go slower, Rachel. Yeah, yeah. You want it in beige but it's red in the photograph? Yeah, I got that. A beige hat. Are you sure they'll have it in beige? Okay, Rachel, don't raise your voice. I'll try. I said I'd try, didn't I? What size? Look, Gladys doesn't go out and buy your presents. Gladys is my secretary. *I* buy your presents. I only meant I've got your sizes somewhere but, look, we've just unpacked and if . . . I only thought if you wanted the hat sent today I'd take everything down an' maybe I'd catch the shops. Rachel, believe me. It would give me the greatest pleasure to get this beige hat for you, if you'd stop interrupting me when I'm trying to get you to describe it. Yeah, Vogue September 1974. I've got that. Is that Paris Vogue or American Vogue? You bought it in London! Is there a London Vogue? Look, if the hat is so pretty damn smart why didn't you fly over from London in September '74 and buy the damn thing? Oh. So you've bought something in beige an' you can't wear it without the hat. Size I've got. Now, Rachel, could you describe it? Look, 'dreamy' is not a description. Does it have a feather? Is it like any other hat I've seen you wear? Look, we could get one made for the price of this call. Of course I want to talk to you. Of course I love you, Rachel. What . . . okay . . . I love you, alright? Sure I miss you, Rachel. Yeah. Fine. I've had a slight touch o' colitis and I haven't been sleeping too good, but never mind. Yeah, Bill's here. Sends his love, Rachel. Rachel, you just don't understand genius. No, I haven't been drinking. Look, can we get back to the hat. Read what it says. Bowler style . Right, so it's a bowler hat. Look, I know what a bowler *hat* is, Rachel. Charlie Chaplin. But this one's in beige but it's red in the photograph. Look, I know you want it in beige. I've got that. Beige. Size 4 and a half. English

Vogue. September '74. I've got all that. The filter system in the pool's not working? Look, Rachel, could we stick to the hat. Phone Ernie about the pool. What can I do about the pool from Paris? I'm sorry, I know swimming's part of your diet. Look, I've always encouraged you in your *diet*, Rachel. I love potatoes. You know how I love potatoes. I haven't eaten one for six and a half years! That's a helluva lot of encouragement, Rachel. Look, just phone Ernie. Ernie knows about pools. That's great. I am enthusiastic. To have lost seven pounds is great. I know you have to swim. Look, go next door to swim. There's a pool next door. Look, there's nothing wrong with your figure. Look, Mrs Bernstein next door is not Miss America. She won't laugh at your body. Christ, Rachel, do you want this goddam bowler hat or don't you? Okay, it's got a scarf tied around it. Why wouldn't you want that scarf? Oh, the scarf matches the red but you want a different scarf to match the beige. Are you sure they do it in . . . I know, all I have to do is ask, Rachel. Where do I ask? Which shop? That one's by Jean Patou but you'd prefer St Laurent . . . the line's better . . . I know you shop there, but isn't a bowler hat — I mean, a beige bowler hat with a different scarf tied around it . . . isn't that seen one seen 'em all? I'll do my best. Yeah. I got the ties for Ernie. I think you think I've all the time in the world to go and buy ties. Sure I like Ernie. I don't dislike him, because he's your brother. That's a lie, Rachel. I never looked down on him because he could fix things. I'm sorry I can't fix television sets. I'm sorry, I don't know how to work the filter system on the pool. Why the hell did you marry me, Rachel? Why didn't you marry a practical man like Ernie? I know he's your brother, and you couldn't marry *him*, but people like Ernie are a dime a dozen. Whattaya mean, 'there I go again'. They *are*. Ernie's a schmuck. Please, Rachel. I'm sorry, I was rude about Ernie. Of course I love you, Rachel. Can we get back to the bowler hat . . . beige, Vogue Magazine, London, September '74, size four and a half, different scarf to match the beige, Patou or St Laurent . . . anything else? There's a brooch on the front of the scarf . . . Look, I'll have to take what brooch is on it, I guess. Look, I don't know whether I'll find that hat yet, so don't give me a bad time about brooches. It's cheap. At St Laurent? Oh, I see . . . the brooch, yeah . . . *looks* cheap. Couldn't *you* change it, Rachel. you got plenty of brooches. You never wear half the things I . . . Whattaya mean I don't take you out where you can dress up . . .? You know I don't like parties. No, Rachel. I am not ashamed of your body. Sure. Once Ernie fixes the pool. Look, it's not my weight that'll give me a heart attack, god-dammit. It's *you*. Rachel, do you hear me? Now, don't talk. Listen. Do you or don't you want this beige bowler hat with the scarf and the brooch? Good. Now, will you accept it with the present brooch or do I buy a beige bowler hat from Patou, a scarf from Yves Saint Laurent and a brooch from Cartier? Just tell me, Rachel. Sure I want to buy it for you. And it won't be a change. Gladys does *not* pick up your presents. Gladys isn't here. Honolulu. On vacation. Now let's not get into Gladys. She has been a good secretary . . . a loyal servant. No, I don't love Gladys Zimmerman. I love Rachel Schneider. Honest.

The lights FADE on the conversation that will only end when either **Walt** *hangs up on Rachel Schneider only to call her back later to apologise or when Rachel hangs up on Walter F. Bickmore and goes to her brother Ernie's house to complain. If it is Walt that hangs up he will know to get her at Ernie's house.*

FADE

SCENE TWO

The suite. Later that evening.

Ford, *wearing Rachel's bowler hat, which pretty well approximates the description in Walt's phone call, sings a song in the centre of the room, having again moved the sofa and slightly re-arranged the furniture.*

Charlie *and* **Wendy** *on the sofa with drinks.* **Chris** *is pouring himself one at the cabinet, while* **Walt** *sits in an armchair, quite*

47

enjoying the song, but a little concerned about the fate of Rachel's hat.

Ford *(singing):*
    I don't feel well at a' the noo
    I ought tae be in bed
    My heart is just as heavy as a hundredweight o' lead
    The cause o' a' the trouble is
    My pair wee Uncle John
    We buried him this mornin'
    It's his claes that I've got on . . . Ah but . . .
    His hat don't fit
    The boots are kinna wee
    I cannae staun the collar
    It nearly strangles me
    I've scarcely room tae breathe it's a fact as death it's true
    The hat's tight. The coat's tight
    And I'm tight too!

    John wisnae much tae look at
    His wis wee by me it's true
    But we were aye the best o' pals
    He stuck tae me like glue
    When aff the booze a nicer chap ye never wished tae see
    But he was never aff the booze
    For he was aye along . . . wi' me . . . Ah but
    His hat don't fit . . .
       He repeats the chorus. **Chris** *and* **Wendy** *join in a little.*
Ford *(singing):*
    The hat's tight. The coat's tight.
    An' I'm tight too!
       They laugh. **Wendy** *claps her hands.* **Ford** *throws the hat to* **Walt** *who catches it, inspects it, and carefully moves it to the top of the television set, far away from* **Ford. Ford** *collapses onto the sofa, beside* **Wendy.**
    Come back, Wendy darlin'. All is forgiven. What d'ye say? Friend?
Wendy: You're a dreadful man.
Ford *(singing):* 'Just friends . . . no lovers we'. That's the stuff.

(He puts his arm round her. A squeeze. She smiles) Back row
o' the pictures, eh, Wendy?

Bick: I hear no typewriters.

Ford: The night is young, Walt. Gie 'im the least wee 'tincture'
o' vodka, Chris. Now, Wendy, how's the wee lassie?

      Chris *pours a vodka for* **Walt.**

Wendy: Caroline?

Ford: Aye.

Wendy: Fine. Reading English. At Cambridge.

Ford: Aye, ye said.

Charlie: Doing very well.

Ford: Cambridge? No red brick for you, eh Charlie?

Chris: You're worse than a snob, Bill. Worse. I was at
Cambridge.

Ford: Wendy, did I say anything against Cambridge? A bit
touchy, isn't ye? Gie Walt 'is potato wine an' behave yersel'.
Oh I see. Jesus pulled the girl of my dreams, is that it?
They're next door.

Wendy: Who?

Ford: Jesus of Nazareth and your au-pair. Well, your *ex* au-pair.
Now, Wendy, that brings me to my point. To make amends
for my wee 'de-trop' last night, where would you like Walt to
take us?

Wendy: No, we can't . . .

Ford: Walt's made o' money. Maxim's?

Wendy: No, honestly. Charlie and I . . . well, we'll leave you to
it.

Ford: Another drink?

Wendy: No. Quite happy, thanks.

Ford: Wendy's happy. You happy, Walt?

Bick: I'd be happier if one of my writers was writing.

Ford: Pointless, Walt. What's the point? Nothin' for you to do
till the rewrite of the rewrite. What ye doin' at the window,
Chris?

Chris: Looking. Quite a crowd.

Ford: Ye see, Wendy, *he* had his eye on her. What d'ye think
she's doin' to Jesus next door, Wendy?

Chris: Piss off.

      There is music from a record player next door. The

Beatles 'Lady Madonna'.

Ford: No cause for alarm, eh, Wendy?

Ford rises and moves over to the window beside **Chris.**

Bick: We got a Jesus listening to 'Lady Madonna', for Christ's sake, with your baby minder from Malmo. Christ, we got a groupie before we got a movie.

Ford: Nil Desperate Dan-dum, Walter.

The sudden sound of rubber bullets and tear gas being fired down in the street.

The music continues from the other room

The young ones at play. The old ones . . . on the beach. And outside the battle rages. And you, Christopher, here you are . . . in the middle, trying to work it all out, to find its significance. Christ, I feel like the country sometimes. On its last fuckin' legs. Sorry, Wendy.

Wendy: I will have another drink, if that's all right.

Bick: Let me. Charlie?

Charlie: Thanks. *(Makes the gesture 'not a large one')*

Walt *takes their glasses and fills them.*

Chris *and* **Ford** *are still at the window, close to the glass, trying to get a better view.*

The sound of tear gas bombs then rubber bullets together. Definite but not too loud.

Chris: Fascists . . .

Ford *(having thought about it):* I hate students. When will they get it into their oversubsidised heads that the workers can't stand them?

Chris: You're such a bringdown, you know that? You really are.

Ford: It was worse in Italy. Louder somehow. 'Course everythin's louder in Italy. Ever done a co-production, Chris?

Chris: Nearly. Once.

Ford: Ye were better away frae it. It was about Sacco and Vanzetti. I don't know what they wanted me for, but you know me, Walter? Refuse nothin' but blows. Anyway, it was typical. You know the form, Italian director, French producer based in Lichtenstein or flying the Liberian flag, cash in hand insisted on, a German cameraman that everybody thought had jumped over the wa', but I know was working for the KGB and an English sound man, slowin' everybody up, but this was different. 'Tally' directors don't shoot dialogue, least this one didn't anyway. He wore a cowboy hat. Thought he was Fellini. Anyway, there they are when I arrive. The Durango Kid havin' tantrums an' a' these actors sayin' numbers or prayers or something. Plenty of gestures but not a syllable of dialogue. It was like a semaphore convention. Anyway, it was the trial scene and there's Sacco or Vanzetti pleading for his life shoutin' 'Twenty-eight. Nine. Eight. One. Three thousand nine hundred and twenty-two. Ave Maria. Ave Maria. Fifty five. Three hundred and ninety an' pater et filio et spiritui sancti' an' after a few minutes o' this the judge bangs his gavil an says: 'Sixteen!' I didnae know what the fuck I was supposed to write so I typed out the ten times table an' pissed off to the airport. You're up here, Chris. Don't worry about down there. Bound to happen in cities. Tear gas bombs. Rubber bullets. Don't add it up to more than that.

Charlie: I'm bankrupt. (*To* **Wendy**) There, I've said it.

Bick: Don't snow me, Charlie.

Wendy: It's true.

Ford: What happened?

Charlie: Agency expanding. Without me, unfortunately. Slimming down. You know? Elbow.

Ford: The bag. The old heave-ho, eh? (**Wendy** *is about to cry*) Now, Wendy. Don't greet.

Wendy: Sorry.

Charlie: Those bastards down there.

Ford: Charlie, come on. Workers, students — whoever they are, they didnae give you the elbow. Brandy's the answer.

> **Ford** *pours* **Charlie** *a large brandy.*

Charlie: Oh, there's a sum of money. A golden handshake, but with my own debts . . . I went into a piece of a few shows, you know? And that's even-steven. Nil. Washed up. What am I going to do, Walt?

Ford: Here's yer brandy.

Charlie: Thanks. Everyone knows. News travels fast in our game.

> *Music from the bedroom.*

Oh, that music!

Ford: Drink the brandy, Charlie. Your client's being well looked after.

Wendy: But he's never done anything else. Well, acting, but even he had to admit . . .

Ford: Never saw ye, Charlie. One of the regrets of my life.

Bick: I could maybe . . . *(A gesture)*

Charlie: No charity, Walt. Thank you, but the answer is no.

Bick: Till you get settled.

Charlie: At what? I started small. Young people. Brought them along. Helped them. Counselled them. I did well, sure, but they did well — at least some of them. If I didn't have a good business the conglomerate wouldn't have wanted to buy me out, would they? I was never happy after that. One day you own a grocers, the next you're serving in the supermarket.

Ford: How ye been getting by?

Charlie: Oh. My wits and . . . good old 'American Express'.

Chris *(looking out):* It's a charge. Night-sticks.

Charlie: I'm glad to be talking about it. You know? Dammit, a lot of people owe a lot to me. The right advice. But they want to run before they can walk. They want to be household names. Stars.

Bick: There are no stars, not any more. Some you pay for aren't even household names in their own house!

Charlie: But try to tell them . . .

Wendy: We can live in a flat. Who needs ten bedrooms? As long as there's a bit of garden.

Ford: Go to my old cottage. The West of Ireland, Charlie. Just the place. Beautiful. Sort yourselves out.

Charlie: People are kind.

Ford: It's just that you've stopped being an agent. There's hope for you yet.

Charlie: Why should you do that for me? Why should I expect your help?

Ford: We're a' in the same boat, that's why. Just listen to us. Ten bedrooms, cottages in paradise, golden handshakes. Walt there's quite keen to find out how much better he'll feel if he gives you a few grand, so you'll be able to keep paying the fees at the golf club and all to the accompaniment of the sounds of battle. It's the bleak time. I've never known a time so . . . BLEAK! The depression was better 'cause we were going to beat it. The war was better 'cause we had a cause and a system, a tyranny to beat. Now, at this moment, nobody has any kind of feeling they're going to beat it. I've made a few bob writing about the working class, but I'm finished anyway, so I don't care much what happens to me or the way we live. I hope I'd be on the streets if I did. 'For the day of his wrath is come. And who shall be able to stand?' My solution was always to go to the nearest bar and wait. But in the meantime, Charlie, you take Wend off to the West of Ireland. It's a better life. Watch the grass grow and wait for the call of the first cuckoo.

Charlie: It must be a blessing to be born not giving a shit.

Wendy: You haven't a care in the world, have you?

Ford: Que sera sera, Wendy.

Charlie: I was never quite respectable.

Ford: It's the tie-pin, Charlie. I know who you are. I don't need your initials on your tie or your cufflinks.

Bick: This is serious, Bill.

Ford: Sorry, Charlie. What are you gonna do?

Charlie: Jump in the Seine.

Wendy: Don't joke. Please.

Charlie: No. The fact is, I don't want to be baled out. I went to the bank. 'You're living beyond your means'. You know how much a bank manager makes? A teller? Peanuts. There was a time I could have bought and sold him. I don't see any point. I don't want to be baled out. What's the point?

Ford: There was a time when there were no cars. A time when there were no cameras. The camera went into the jungle and photographed the natives. Their rituals. Nothing was as pure and simple after that. The camera took their rituals. Once they had been recorded there was no need to celebrate them. The camera took their dances, their rituals, their magic and the motor car will takes their lives. There was a thatcher. A thatcher for Christ's sake, but this was only last year, I'm talkin' about. Only last year. In the West. This thatcher called Niall. He died. Murdered by a stranger. In a car. And Niall came there. Was born there. Before cars. When the fields were stones and he cleared every stone to find the *land*.

He tilled the land. But the car took him. Right outside my house it was. Dressed in a new suit. Brand new. We buried him in it. That suit cost him his land. The local shopkeeper … the local 'gombeen man' encouraged him to buy things. What does a thatcher need wi' a three piece suit? You don't need to dress up for mass in the country. Christ! Givin' beads and firewater to the fuckin' Indians wisnae in it. He claimed every stone. Made things grow. On the land. It's a site for a factory now. The bastard got seventy five grand for it. They make plastic donkeys and . . . would you believe . . . plastic thatched cottages wi' 'Erin go Bragh' on the door? So don't be surprised, Wendy, if I don't give *that* much for your economic crisis. Are you really surprised there are students or workers or whoever they are fightin' the polis down there? Are ye? *(Music from the next room.)*

Bick: An' you kids shut up, Hear? *(The music fades down a bit)* I got the blues. Honest, Charlie, I wish you'd never come.

Wendy: That's what I said. Let's go. *(She rises)*

Ford: Sit down, Wendy. Walt doesnae mean it. Chris, what's the matter wi' you? Maybe *you* could lend Charlie a few bob?

Charlie: I don't think that's very funny.

Chris: Should we go down?

Ford: Pour me a brandy first, Chris. You're there, Walt. D'ye mind. Insulation. There's still a nip in the air.

Charlie: Don't go. I don't know what to do. I'm asking your advice.

Wendy: It's my fault. I'm not really like this, you know. I'm fat. Yes, fat. I was a fat girl. Always. Diets. Health farms, trying to impress people. Trying to help my husband be a success. It's my fault. I must have cost you a fortune.

Bick: Wives cost a fortune. It's the price you pay, that's all. Don't get me started. You see that hat? *(He lifts Rachel's hat)* The price o' that hat could nearly bale you out, Charlie.

Chris: I want to go down. Is anybody coming?

Ford: I wonder if this is . . . *it*.

Charlie: Mind if I join you?

Ford: Aye. You come, Charlie. Take your mind off your overdraft.

Charlie: Wendy?

Wendy: I'll wait. Don't be long. I'm tired.

Charlie: Won't be long, darling.

Bick: Would you do me a favour, Wendy?

Wendy: What's that?

Bick: Try Rachel's hat on.

Wendy: It's sweet.

Ford: What about the carpenter's son?

Chris: Oh, leave them.

> **Wendy** *is by a mirror changing the angle of the hat on her head.*

Charlie: Wendy . . .

Wendy: Do you like it?

Charlie: It's funny.

Wendy: Well!

Charlie: I'll take a photograph. *(Mimes taking his photograph)* Click!

> *Then,* **Ford, Chris** *and* **Charlie** *leave by the main door.*

Bick: It'll suit Rachel. She's fat. I mean, she's really fat. I hope she likes it. Anything for a quiet life. Thank you.

> **Wendy** *takes off the hat. She sits down.*

And don't worry about Charlie. He'll be alright.

Wendy: But what'll he do?

Bick: He'll be alright, I tell ya.

Wendy: But that's favours, Walter.

Bick: Doing a guy a favour never hurt nobody.

Wendy: Maybe it would hurt him. You don't know him, Walter. Not really, He wants to be in charge. The boss, you know? It doesn't have to be big business as long as he's the boss.

Bick: I'll give him a good salary and a fancy title. People won't know a thing. Back on his feet. He can start again.

Wendy: You're kind.

Bick: Yeah.

Wendy: How did we get caught? What did we do that we could have done different? Why aren't we happy?

Bick: Hey, Ralphy! Play some bad music. Real loud.

> **Agneta** *comes to the door of the bedroom.*

Hi, kid. Wendy and I are gonna dance.

Ralph *comes to the bedroom door. He puts his arm around* **Agneta**.

Bick: Ralphy boy, I was just saying to the girl here that Wendy and I are gonna dance. Now this dance will be somewhat subdued and lacking in energy compared to the dancing you've maybe got in mind, so I would like you to choose an appropriate accompaniment. There was a time when Jolson singing 'The Anniversary Waltz' would have filled the bill, or 'Moonlight Serenade' or 'Don't Sit Under the Apple Tree with Anyone Else But Me' would have been ideal, but those days are gone, so we'll fit our twinkle steps to whatever the band in there would like to play. Samba? Rhumba? We're game for anything. So take your partners, Wendy.

> **Wendy** *rises and joins him in the centre of the room.*
>
> **Ralph** *goes off to play the record.*
>
> **Walt** *brings* **Wendy** *close to him. The music begins: Stevie Winwood's 'Dear Mr Fantasy' sung by Al Kooper and Mike Bloomfield. The couple dance cheek to cheek. Another tear gas bomb in the distance. The loudest yet. Then the music is turned up so that it is quite loud in the main room.*
>
> **Ralph** *comes out and dances, groping* **Agneta,** *the while.*
>
> **Walt** *insists on the grip and the Astaire steps of the ballrooms of his youth. You feel that once he did competitions with a number on his back, partnered by a sequined Rachel Schneider.* **Wendy** *also dances with grace and technique.*
>
> **Ralph** *and* **Agneta** *neck mostly. They eventually retire to the corner of the suite leaving the floor to* **Walt** *and* **Wendy** *as the organ swells on the record:*

Dear Mr Fantasy
Play us a tune
Somethin' to make us all happy
Do anything
Take us out of this gloom
Sing a song, play guitar
Make it snappy.

> *The organ swells on the record.*
>
> *The main door opens.* **Chris** *comes in and goes quickly to the drinks cabinet. A few moments later* **Ford** *enters.*

He stands by the main door watching the Dancers. **Wendy** and **Walt** put on just a little extra for his benefit.
Ford slowly, carefully buttons his collar, straightens his tie and walks between the Dancers.

Ford: This is an 'excuse me'. May I cut in?

Bick: My pleasure, young man.

Ford begins to dance cheek to cheek with **Wendy**. **Walt**, a bit pooped, goes over to the drinks cabinet. He squirts some soda water into a glass. **Chris** puts his arm around his shoulder.

Chris (quietly, matter of fact): Charlie threw himself under a taxi. He's all over the street.

Ford (to **Wendy**): Tripping the light fantastic, eh Wendy? The light fantastic.

Ford holds her tight. 'Dear Mr Fantasy' blares on.

FADE

SCENE THREE

Blazing white light.

Technicans enter and after a bang on the wall and a shout of 'Lose the wall' begin to dismantle the set. This reveals lights, cables, a Panaflex camera on a dolly and all the paraphernalia of a film studio at work.

The movie is being made. A year of changes, rewrites and frustration has passed. We are now in a London film studio on the 'Paris Hotel Suite' set. A bell rings. There is suddenly less light as the **Technicians** leave the stage empty for a time.

Then **Ralph** enters. He is in his costume and make-up as **Jesus** — long hair, beard, white robe, crown of thorns — the lot. He *pulls a canvas chair to near the centre of the stage 'in' the room. He sits down. He reaches to his crutch under the robe and pulls out a reasonably good rather big cigar. He lights it from a table lighter on the 'set' and smokes it with the band on.*

Ford *comes in. He carries a script in a loose-leaf folder which he is peering at through gold half-glasses. He goes to the drinks table. He pours a large scotch and as usual, carefully tops it up with his measure of water. He takes a gulp. Suddenly, he spits it out all over the carpet.*

Ford: Christ! Water an' burnt sugar or mixed with shite or somethin'.

> *He grimaces then takes a leather covered hip flask out of his jacket pocket. He takes another glass from the drinks cabinet and pours a real drink.*

Serves me right for being mean.

> *He sips his drink, as he walks around the room, past* **Ralph** *who sits reading 'Oui'. Eventually,* **Ford** *stands behind* **Ralph.** *He is in a fixed stare as* **Ralph** *turns the pages.*

What's it supposed to be?

Ralph *(reading):* 'A frank photographic essay, based on the last speech of James Joyce's immortal classic "Ulysses" with Bibi Borgen as Molly Bloom conceived, directed and photographed by Just Jaeckin'.

Ford: Dirty bastard! I brought it back from Paris, you know. First edition. Two volumes. Shakespeare and Company. I was going to Dublin. Smuggled it in. You must realise they were ex-communicatin' folk for readin' Joyce in those days. Anyway I gave the first volume to a mate o' mine. An actor. Liam Redmond.

Ralph: I know him. Very good.

Ford: Sure. Anyway, the next night Liam comes bangin' on my door demanding volume two. 'I'm only a half educated man', says he. Quite good.

Ralph: How is he? *(Turning pages)* Would you look at these knockers!

Ford: Oh, Liam's ace. A one. He goes round Dublin tellin' stories an' jokes an' . . . you know. If he gets a laugh he says nothin', if he's greeted with stony silence he says 'Bill Ford told me that one.' That's Friends for you. You any friends, Ralph? Hey, I'm not so sure that's proper readin' for saviours. Gie's it.

Ralph: Piss off.

    Slight pause.

Ford: Big chance for you, this.

Ralph: Yeah.

Ford: Holidays with pay for the likes o' me. Paris. Morocco an' here we are in rural Shepperton, an' I'm livin' above my favourite restaurant.

Ralph: You at the Connaught?

Ford: Where else?

Ralph: You didn't see much of Morocco.

Ford: Unfortunate.

Ralph: You left Chris in the shit.

Ford: Sure. If I hadn't, he'd still be here wastin' his time. I'm too old to worry about translatin' Italian rubbish into English rubbish. Chris has his whole life in front of him. He's writin' a play, so I hear. Look, Ralph, I'm immortal. What's your excuse?

Ralph: Don't worry about me. If this is a balls-up, I'll get a job.

Ford: I'm not worried about *you,* Ralph.

    Pause. Ford *moves back to the drinks cabinet and puts a fraction more water in his whisky.*

    I wrote a poem last night.

Ralph: Oh yeah.

Ford: *Oh yeah.* I thought I was finished. Christ, I am finished. Nevertheless . . . I wrote a poem last night.

Ralph: Pretty chuffed, eh?

Ford: I wrote a poem. Of course, I'm fuckin' chuffed. How's the wee girl? ye heard?

Ralph: Sorry?

Ford: Agneta? How's she doin'?

Ralph: She wrote. I haven't replied.

Ford: You're daft.

Ralph: Look, Bill, I've got enough problems.

Ford: What are ye? Thirty. Thirty-two? Problems? You haven't replied to a *blessing,* Ralphy boy. If I had anythin' to offer her apart from a black veil at a funeral, I'd be on the next plane to wherever the hell she is, to take her back to wherever I was and I'd stay if she didn't want to move. That's one in a million you haven't replied to, and you'll live to regret it. You'll be like everybody else in your misfortune. You'll be so famous you'll need one of these over educated under-sexed amazingly fertile, American ex-groupies to mother you through your notoriety. God help ye. Here's Walt.

Walt *enters. He carries a carton of coffee and a script.*

Bick: That tight arsed little *Italian* faggot is fucking me up!

Ford: I've heard ye say that about most nationalities, Walt.

Bick: I've worked under Selznick. I worked under Harry Cohn, for Christ's sake, before I made a buck and I always got it.

Ford: What ye talkin' about, Walt?

Bick: 'Mr *Bickmore's* rehearsal'. I'm in my office. It doesn't matter a fuck where I am. A bell rings when they're ready to shoot a scene. A bell rings and I come down on the floor and that's 'Mr *Bickmore's* rehearsal'. I give my notes on that and when the notes are put in they can shoot it. That's the way it was. But this little Gucci shoed asshole. . .

Ford: The way it was, Walt. The way it was. You hired him?

Bick: He was hot.

Ford: He talks like Visconti an' directs like Vadim

Ralph: He's a very talented man.

Bick: Shut up, kid, or I'll cut you out the picture.

Ford: 'Why do you want all the disciples to be poofs?' says I. 'Why else would they follow Him?', says he.

    Slight pause.

Bick: Keach is very good. Saw some rushes. Look, kid, could you go to your room. Sorry. We're in conference.

Ralph: Sure. Anything I can do?

Bick: Yeah. Piss off. Sorry. You're doing a great job, kid. You're gonna be a star. Later, okay. It's a great motion picture.

Bick: Yeah. See ya, kid.

Ford: All the best.

    Ralph *rises and walks through the wall of the set, past the camera and out of sight.*

Bick: I can't get 'im off the picture.

Ford: Who? The regista. 'Il poeta'. 'Il maestro'.

Bick: Il pain in the ass.

Ford: Tough.

Bick: Oh, we'll salvage something. Like always.

Ford: Never had much to do with quality, have we, Walt?

Bick: We've had a few laughs.

Ford: Without question. Don't get me wrong.

Bick: How do we always . . . get caught? You feel it comin'. You start off an' you've everything goin' for you. The recipe for success. Then you feel it slip away. How does it happen? You're caught. Trapped. It's never like you hoped.

Ford: There's no recipe for success, Walt. Only for failure. And that's tryin' to please everybody.

Bick: You're some help. Sittin' there . . . philosophisin'. It ain't *Your* ass, Bill.

Ford: No. It ain't my ass, Walt.

Bick: It's just another 'Jesus' picture. All the stuff we shot about the preparation an' the crew and the life around a movie. All *your* stuff. It'll be in the trashcan. Il dope-o didn't shoot it right. Front office'll back him. His last picture's doin' figures everywhere. Oh, Christ!

Ford: *He* won't help you now, Walt. Don't worry about me. I'm used to ending up in the trashcan. I should have kept my mouth shut an' got on with it.

   Pause.

Bick: It's cold.

Ford: They turned the lights off.

Bick: Spooky. A waste o' money, this set. Waste o' money.

Ford: Sorry, Walt. I'd offer ye a drink, but the vodka might be paint thinners.

Bick: What are we gonna do, Bill?

Ford: You'll ring Santillo. Get him to re-cut the picture.

Bick: He's free.

Ford: There's you versus 'the tally' an' he's so hot that even if you pissed on him he wouldn't go out. You'll either fight him and the studio and the Directors Guild, or you'll sit back and pray that twenty million dollars worth of admissions still have time for Jesus. I'm going home.

Bick: How's Sarah?

Ford: I don't know. It's that long since I've seen her. I don't know whether it was a compliment or not, but last week, on the phone, she said: "It's so good here when there's no excitements". It's wonderful to be thought of as an excitement. But I miss the grandchildren.

Bick: Rachel couldn't have kids. So the doctor said.

Ford: Saved you the problem of nepotism, Walt. Cost you a way out.

Bick: What?

Ford: We're on the beach, Walt. Whales. The gran' weans is the cat's pajamas. You can spoil them without feeling any guilt. Remarkable, mine. The oldest, he was here in London last year. Notting Hill. Lots of blacks in the market one Saturday. I feared the worst. You know? 'Why is that man black, grandad?' All that. But nothing. A week later back in Glasgow. An American sailor. He came up to us in Sauchiehall Street. Gave the boy a bar of chocolate. William took it. I waited for the spade jokes. Nothing. 'That's a man from London', he said. There are more important things than worry about some jumped up arse-hole fuckin' you up. You've made enough dough.

Bick: What else can I do?

Ford: That's crap. If nobody published me, I'd be in the shipyard like everybody else.

Bick: I'd 'a been a lawyer.

Ford: You don't give the impression of being educated, Walt. I'm not educated, but I'm given the benefit of the doubt. You are, but everyone presumes you came out of the womb waving a contract for the mechanical rights in case it was the immaculate conception. It's hard to imagine you young, Walt.

Bick: You, too.

Ford: Aye. We're old. Passed it.

> *Pause.*

Bick: Why should I fight it? Nobody expected integrity before, why should I deliver it now? Let them have a Jesus picture that's what they expect of me, isn't it? Christ, I did my first picture with Bill Wellman, my second with Raoul Walsh. I'm the old movies, so you say. So give 'em an old movie an' what the fuck's the difference? I could retire good. Take Rachel to Florida. She likes Florida.

Ford: Write your memoirs.

Bick: I don't need to do that. Some Frog critic will discover me. Look at Nick Ray, Howard Hawks . . . all of 'em. Jerry Lewis, for Christ's sake!!

Ford: Be a 'grand old man' like me, Walt.

Bick: Whales.

Ford: Look at us. We're rich men. People'll say we're cryin' all the way to the bank.

Bick: We haven't done much but some people haven't done anything.

> **Ford** *takes out his hip flask. He fills his glass.*
> **Walt** *reaches for* **Ford** *gives it to him.* **Walt** *drinks from it.*

Just this once. *(He takes a short sip)*

Ford: Cheers, Walt. Here's tae your retirement and let's hope that not too many of your movies stink on television. Time heals.

Bick: Remember . . .

Ford: Don't start, Walt.

Bick: No.

Ford: When I wrote my first novel the publisher found out that for a week I'd been on the night-shift guarding the distillery. Perfect casting. No, but anyway he found this out so the blurb said: 'William Ford: ex-sailor, pastry cook, circus ringmaster and fisherman wrote this novel while working on the night-shift'. I felt sorry for myself goin' through a' that for three hundred indulgent pages about my old man and the strike, but there it was. Did I deny it? No. So there I am with students getting double firsts in modern literature finding out what sacrifice means, and worse. Poor bastards signing on for the night shift in the hope that their first novel will dawn on them at half-three in the mornin' when the alsatians stopped tryin' to find burglars to maul.

> **Walt** *takes a swig out of the hip flask.*

Bick: What am I doing? Following trends. A shark picture makes a fortune, so I try to buy up all the shark books. It was the Mafia before an' I go to Italy an' make two Mafia movies back to back. Well, not me. My company. I'm so ashamed of the rip-off I won't even sign the damn thing. Christ, if Bambi was big news I'd have signed up every antelope in Africa.

Ford: Was Bambi an antelope?

Bick: How do I know?

Ford: Just wondered. 'Man is in the forest, Bambi'. Best line in the movies.

Bick: 'Frankly, my dear, I don't give a damn.'

Ford: 'We have the stars'.

Bick: I wish to God we did. How can schmucks succeed an' guys like you an' me not make it. How?

Ford: 'If you want me. Whistle'.

Bick: Alright. 'I coulda been a contender, Charlie.'

Ford: 'Well, nobody's perfect'.

Bick: 'I taught I taw a puddy cat'.

Ford *(as Gabby Hayes):* 'Jumpin' Jehosephat, Hoppy!

Bick: 'A good laugh may not be much but it's all some people get in this cockeyed caravan. Boy!'

     They both laugh.

Ford: If this was the theatre it would be different. Every night. A different inflection. Tone. Slightly different timing. That film down there is locked. For good, or ill, it's locked. You win. You lose. Who cares, Walt? I'm sorry for my idea. I'm sorry I found us interesting.

Bick: We ain't dead yet.

Ford *(impersonating* **Walt***)*: Bet your ass.

Ford: We're in a set. Men built it. They're more interesting than some fag with a free Ferrari. Sid!!

     A Voice *from the flies responds.*

There's Sid. *(Half addressing the flies)* I move up to this light switch. And Sid's there. I don't turn it off. I put my hand round it and hope that Sid's there and it's off.

The main light in the room goes out.

Bick: What?

Ford: It's the only magic left.

Bick: What are you trying to pull?

Ford: We'll settle for half, Walt. We'll settle for the market place. We'll settle for the 'Eau-Sauvaged' Florentine. But here's *magic*. The lights are out. The set. Well, that's just canvas. Paint. An' the whisky is burnt sugar. The gin and the vodka are paint thinners or worse. The creme de menthe is cough mixture. It's all a phony, so we were better away frae it. But Sid up there, he'll never get away frae it. Sid's there so when you put your hand to the switch, the lights go out and . . . when the time comes *(he looks above him)* The curtain falls.

THE CURTAIN FALLS